Colony of Heaven
A Fresh Look at Ephesians

James J. Burke

Fireproof Commentaries

Volume II

FIREPROOF
COMMENTARIES

ISBN-13: — 979-8-9941637-1-9

All Scripture quotations from the King James Version unless otherwise specified

Printed in the United States of America

fireproofcommentaries.org

To my Mom — who quietly built a colony of heaven at our kitchen table and front porch, shaping fireproof hearts, even when we resisted. Her faithful labor became the soil from which this book grew.

Table of Contents

Foreword

When I first began studying the Epistle to the Ephesians, I was struck by how Paul refuses to let the church think of itself as a loose gathering of individuals. Instead, he paints a picture of the church as an outpost of heaven—an embassy of Christ's kingdom planted in a world estranged from God. That vision has shaped my preaching, my pastoring, and my writing for years.

This book, Colony of Heaven, grew out of my sermons, studies, and countless conversations with believers who want to understand their place in God's plan. Like my first volume, Building a Fireproof Church, it is both a commentary and a call to action. My goal is not merely to inform your mind but to stir your heart and strengthen your walk with Christ. Each chapter follows a simple pattern—exposition, summary, application, and prayer—so that individuals, small groups, and entire congregations can grow together in their understanding and practice of Scripture.

As you work through these pages, you will find the recurring theme of "Colony of Heaven." This is more than a title. It's an identity. We are not waiting for the day we escape to a distant city; we are already citizens of that city now, called to bring its culture, values, and beauty into our neighborhoods, workplaces, and families. My hope is that this book will help you see the grandeur of Christ's calling, the richness of His grace, and the power of His Spirit at work in you.

To my readers—pastors, parents, teens, and new believers alike—thank you for letting me walk alongside you through this letter of Paul's. May the Spirit of God open your eyes to the hope of His calling, deepen your roots in Christ, and give you courage to live as a citizen of heaven's colony, right where He has placed you.

— James J. Burke

Marinette, Wisconsin

2025

Preface: Colony of Heaven

In the ancient world, Roman colonies were remarkable outposts of civilization, planted in distant and often untamed lands. These colonies were not mere settlements; they were strategic extensions of the home city, designed to embody and express its culture, laws, and values amidst foreign territories. Cities like Philippi, Corinth, or Antioch were established as microcosms of Rome, carrying the prestige and identity of their founding metropolis. They stood as beacons of order and influence in regions often considered barbarian, transforming their surroundings by radiating the ethos of the home city.

For the citizens of these colonies, their identity was rooted not in a longing to relocate to the home city—a place most had never seen and likely never would—but in the privilege and responsibility of representing it. Their citizenship was not a ticket to a distant capital but a calling to live out the values, language, and customs of that city in their local context. They were ambassadors of a greater reality, tasked with making the home city's presence felt in every aspect of their lives, from governance to daily interactions.

The Apostle Paul, writing to the churches of Asia Minor, presents the church as a *Colony of Heaven*—a community of believers called to be an outpost of

Colony of Heaven

God's kingdom in a world estranged from Him. In this epistle, Paul unfolds the breathtaking reality of our citizenship in Christ, not as a future hope of escape to a heavenly city, but as a present vocation to embody the culture of heaven here and now. As citizens of this divine colony, we are not merely waiting to "go home"; we are commissioned to represent our King, to live out His grace, truth, and love in a world that desperately needs to see His light.

This devotional commentary, *Colony of Heaven*, explores the Epistle to the Ephesians as a manifesto for living as God's outpost in the world. Through Paul's inspired words, we will uncover what it means to be rooted in Christ's redemptive work, equipped by His Spirit, and sent to display the beauty of heaven's kingdom in our relationships, communities, and daily lives. My prayer is that this journey through Ephesians will inspire and empower you to embrace your calling as a citizen of heaven's colony, faithfully representing our eternal home in a world longing for its hope.

1

Citizens of Heaven's Colony

The Epistle to the Ephesians is a treasure of divine revelation, a letter that unveils the grandeur of God's plan for His people and the world. It is not a letter addressing a single church's struggles or a specific doctrinal error, as we see in Paul's letters to Corinth or Colossae. Instead, Ephesians is an **encyclical** —a letter meant for multiple churches, carried by Tychicus with a blank space for the name of each recipient congregation (Eph. 6:21–22). Some ancient manuscripts address it to Ephesus, others to Laodicea, and some leave the destination blank, underscoring its universal message (Metzger, 1994). If any book in the New Testament could be said to be written to every church, including ours today, it is Ephesians. It is a timeless

> **Why This Letter Matters Everywhere**
>
> *Ephesians circulated as an* **encyclical***, not a single-church letter. Because its message was meant for every congregation, this commentary emphasizes timeless truths over local Ephesian details, showing how Paul's call to live as a "Colony of Heaven" applies in any place and era.*

manifesto of the gospel's truth and its transformative impact on our lives.

The city of Ephesus was a hub of commerce, culture, and religion in the ancient world. Paul spent two years there, teaching in the school of Tyrannus and sparking a spiritual awakening that reverberated across Asia Minor (Acts 19:9–10). His ministry was so impactful that it provoked a riot from those who feared the gospel's threat to their idol-worshipping economy, shouting, "Great is Diana of the Ephesians!" (Acts 19:28, KJV).   Even after Paul's departure, Ephesus remained a center of Christian influence, hosting the Apostle John before his sojourn on Patmos (Eusebius, Church History, 3.23). Yet, despite Paul's deep connection to Ephesus, this letter contains no personal greetings or specific references to individuals, unlike Romans 16 or Colossians 4. Why? Because Ephesians was written not to address local issues but to proclaim the universal calling of the church as God's outpost in the world—a Colony of Heaven.

Written during Paul's imprisonment, likely in Rome in the early 60s A.D. (Bruce, 1984), Ephesians is a mature expression of his theology. Alongside Philippians, Colossians, and Philemon, it forms the Prison Epistles, penned while Paul was under house arrest, awaiting trial before Caesar (Acts 28:30–31). Some scholars propose an earlier imprisonment in

Caesarea or even an unrecorded imprisonment in Ephesus (Clement of Alexandria, Stromata, 4.8), but the traditional view of a Roman origin best fits the historical and textual evidence (O'Brien, 1999). Carried by Tychicus, who also delivered letters to Colossae and Philemon (Col. 4:7–9), Ephesians outlines God's cosmic plan in Christ and the church's role in displaying it. The first three chapters are doctrinal, grounding us in the truth of our salvation; the last three are practical, showing how that truth shapes our lives.

Ephesians 1 is a breathtaking overture, introducing the theme that will resound throughout the letter: it's all about Christ, not us. As citizens of heaven's colony, we are not saved because of our merit or uniqueness but to display God's glory in Christ. This chapter unfolds the hope of His calling, the riches of our inheritance, and the incomparable greatness of His power, inviting us to live as representatives of our heavenly King.

> *Paul, an apostle of Jesus Christ by the will of God, to the saints which are at Ephesus, and to the faithful in Christ Jesus: Grace be to you, and peace, from God our Father, and from the Lord Jesus Christ. Blessed be the God and Father of our Lord Jesus Christ, who hath blessed us with all spiritual blessings in heavenly places in Christ: According as he*

hath chosen us in him before the foundation of the world, that we should be holy and without blame before him in love: Having predestinated us unto the adoption of children by Jesus Christ to himself, according to the good pleasure of his will, To the praise of the glory of his grace, wherein he hath made us accepted in the beloved. In whom we have redemption through his blood, the forgiveness of sins, according to the riches of his grace; Wherein he hath abounded toward us in all wisdom and prudence; Having made known unto us the mystery of his will, according to his good pleasure which he hath purposed in himself: That in the dispensation of the fulness of times he might gather together in one all things in Christ, both which are in heaven, and which are on earth; even in him: In whom also we have obtained an inheritance, being predestinated according to the purpose of him who worketh all things after the counsel of his own will: That we should be to the praise of his glory, who first trusted in Christ. In whom ye also trusted, after that ye heard the word of truth, the gospel of your salvation: in whom also after that ye believed, ye were sealed with that holy Spirit of promise, Which is the earnest of our inheritance until the redemption of the purchased possession, unto the praise of his glory. (Ephesians 1:1-14 KJV)

The Hope of His Calling (Ephesians 1:1–14)

Paul begins, "Paul, an apostle of Jesus Christ by the will of God, to the saints which are at Ephesus, and to the faithful in Christ Jesus: Grace be to you, and peace, from God our Father, and from the Lord Jesus Christ" (Eph. 1:1–2, KJV). These opening words establish the tone of divine grace and the centrality of Christ. The recipients are "saints" and "faithful in Christ Jesus"—terms that describe not only the believers in Ephesus but all who are united to Christ by faith. As citizens of heaven's colony, we are set apart, called to represent our King in a foreign land.

Saints

Saint is never singular in the New Testament, it always is used for the church collectively.

Verses 3–14 form a single, majestic sentence in the Greek, a cascade of praise for God's work in Christ. Paul declares, "Blessed be the God and Father of our Lord Jesus Christ, who hath blessed us with all spiritual blessings in heavenly places in Christ" (Eph. 1:3, KJV). Every spiritual blessing—redemption, adoption, forgiveness—flows to us through our union with Christ. This is the foundation of our citizenship: we are "in Christ," a phrase Paul uses repeatedly to emphasize that our identity and purpose are rooted in Him.

Chosen and Predestined for God's Glory

Paul then unveils the doctrine of election: "According as he hath chosen us in him before the foundation of the world, that we should be holy and without blame before him in love" (Eph. 1:4, KJV). This verse has sparked much debate, but its meaning is not about God arbitrarily selecting some for salvation and others for condemnation. Rather, it affirms that all who are in Christ are chosen for a purpose: to be holy and blameless. Holiness is sanctification—being set apart for God's service. To be blameless is to live in a way that does not tarnish Christ's reputation. As citizens of heaven's colony, we are not chosen for privilege alone but for responsibility—to reflect the character of our King.

> **For a deeper discussion of predestination, see Appendix A: Predestination: Privilege or Purpose?**

This choosing is not about excluding others but about equipping us for a divine mission. Paul continues, "Having predestinated us unto the adoption of children by Jesus Christ to himself, according to the good pleasure of his will" (Eph. 1:5, KJV). Predestination is not a cold, deterministic decree but a loving act of God's will, securing our place in His family. Adoption in the Roman world was a legal act, granting full rights as heirs (Sherwin-White, 1963). As God's adopted children, we are heirs today, not merely in the future. Our inheritance is our new position in His family, sealed by redemption: "In whom we have redemption through his blood, the forgiveness of sins, according to the riches of his grace" (Eph. 1:7, KJV).

Chosen as Representatives

To grasp the weight of being "chosen in Christ," consider the ancient practice of establishing Roman colonies. These outposts, like Philippi or Corinth, were carefully planned to extend the home city's culture, laws, and influence into foreign territories (Boardman, 1980). Colonists were not chosen randomly; they were selected for their loyalty, skills, and ability to embody the home city's values. In Rome, veterans who had proven their allegiance through military service were often granted land in colonies, ensuring they would uphold Roman law and customs (Salmon, 1969). In Greek colonies, settlers were chosen for their agricultural or administrative expertise to sustain the settlement and reflect the mother city's glory (Graham, 1983). These colonists were not sent to assimilate into local "barbarian" cultures but to transform their surroundings by establishing the home city's institutions—temples, forums, and legal systems

—making places like Philippi a "little Rome" in Macedonia (Acts 16:12; Levick, 1967).

Crucially, these colonists did not dream of relocating to the home city, which most had never seen. Their citizenship was a calling to represent their city's greatness where they were, living as ambassadors of its culture and authority. Likewise, God has chosen us in Christ "before the foundation of the world" (Eph. 1:4, KJV) not to escape to heaven but to represent His kingdom on earth. We are selected not for our inherent worth but for His purpose—to be holy and blameless, displaying His glory in a world estranged from Him. Just as colonists were equipped with resources and instructions to succeed, God equips us with "all spiritual blessings" (Eph. 1:3, KJV) and the Holy Spirit as the "earnest of our inheritance" (Eph. 1:14, KJV), ensuring we can live out our calling.

This selection carries a responsibility. As Roman colonists were expected to live in a way that honored Rome, we must live in a way that honors Christ. People should look at us and see the beauty of His kingdom, not stumble over our inconsistencies and say, "You claim to be holy, but your actions say otherwise." Our lives are to reflect the priorities of our King, transforming our communities through love, truth, and godliness, just as a colony transformed its region by radiating the home city's culture.

Redemption underscores this transformative purpose. Imagine driftwood washed up on a lakeshore—some see it as trash, fit only for burning, but an artist sees potential for beauty. God takes us, broken and without inherent value, and assigns us worth through Christ's blood. He reshapes us into the image of His Son, crafting us for His purpose. Every trial, every correction, every blessing in our lives is part of His plan to display Christ's lordship. Paul writes that God's ultimate will is "that in the dispensation of the fulness of times he might gather together in one all things in Christ, both which are in heaven, and which are on earth" (Eph. 1:10, KJV). Our lives, as citizens of heaven's colony, are display pieces of this cosmic plan, showing the world that Christ is Lord over all.

Dispensation

For definition of dispensation and other unfamiliar terms, check the glossary

Three times in this passage, Paul emphasizes that our salvation is "to the praise of his glory" (Eph. 1:6, 12, 14, KJV). God did not save us because He needed us or because we were inherently special. He saved us to showcase His greatness. Our adoption, the revelation of His will, and the sealing of the Holy Spirit as the "earnest of our inheritance" (Eph. 1:14, KJV) all point to His glory, not ours. The Spirit is the down payment, guaranteeing our full redemption as God's possession. As citizens, we live not for our own

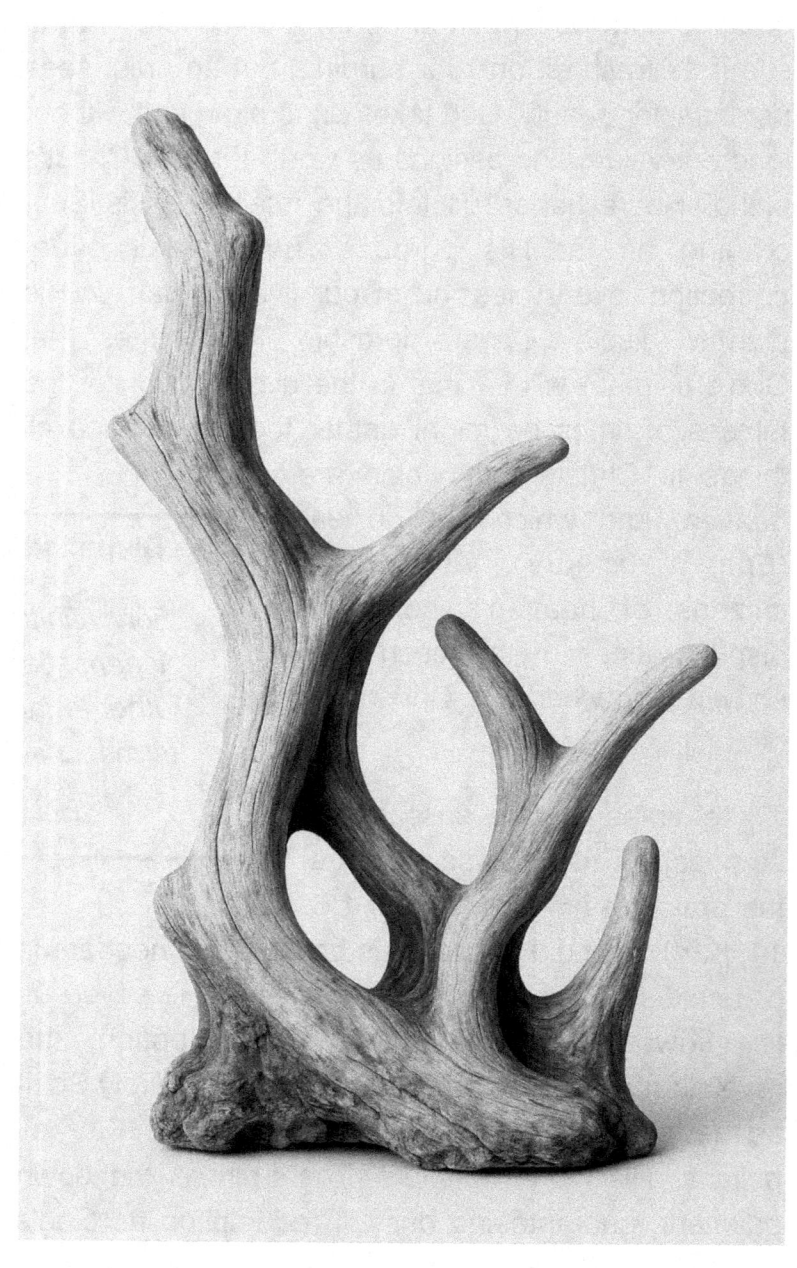

acclaim but to reflect the splendor of our King.

The Riches of Our Inheritance (Ephesians 1:15–18)

Paul transitions to a prayer: "Wherefore I also, after I heard of your faith in the Lord Jesus, and love unto all the saints, cease not to give thanks for you, making mention of you in my prayers" (Eph. 1:15–16, KJV). He prays that God would grant them "the spirit of wisdom and revelation in the knowledge of him" (Eph. 1:17, KJV). This is not mere intellectual knowledge but a growing, experiential understanding of God's character and plan. As citizens of heaven's colony, we need spiritual insight to grasp our role in His kingdom.

Paul's prayer focuses on three realities: the hope of God's calling, the riches of His inheritance in the saints, and the greatness of His power (Eph. 1:18–19). The hope of His calling is the certainty of our purpose—to be holy and blameless, representing Christ. The inheritance is not only what we receive but what God receives in us—His people, redeemed to display His glory (O'Brien, 1999). As a sculptor values a masterpiece not for the raw material but for the beauty crafted from it, God treasures us as His workmanship, shaped for His purposes.

The Incomparable Greatness of His Power (Ephesians 1:19–23)

The third focus of Paul's prayer is "the exceeding greatness of his power to us-ward who believe, according to the working of his mighty power, which he wrought in Christ, when he raised him from the dead, and set him at his own right hand in the heavenly places" (Eph. 1:19–20, KJV). The same power that raised Jesus from the dead and exalted Him above all powers is at work in us. This is no ordinary strength; it is divine, resurrection power, enabling us to live as faithful citizens of heaven's colony.

Paul concludes, "And hath put all things under his feet, and gave him to be the head over all things to the church, which is his body, the fulness of him that filleth all in all" (Eph. 1:22–23, KJV). Christ is the head, and the church is His body—the visible expression of His rule and presence on earth. The term "head" carries profound meaning, revealing Christ as both our leader and our source, shaping our calling as God's colony.

As our leader, Christ exercises supreme authority over the church and all creation. Just as a Roman colony looked to the emperor or governor for direction, submitting to Rome's laws to reflect its authority, the church submits to Christ's sovereign rule. He is exalted "far above all principality, and power, and might, and dominion" (Eph. 1:21, KJV), and as His body, we are called to display His preeminence. Our relationships, decisions, and actions should reflect a community where Christ reigns, radiating His love, justice, and grace to a watching world.

As our source, Christ is the origin of the church's life and mission. In ancient thought, the head was seen as the source of vitality for the body, supplying nourishment and direction (Hoehner, 2002). Likewise, Christ fills the church—His "fulness"—with His Spirit, grace, and power, enabling us to embody His kingdom. Just as a Roman colony depended on the home city for its culture, laws, and resources, we draw our identity and strength from Christ. The "spiritual blessings" of redemption, adoption, and the Holy Spirit (Eph. 1:3–14, KJV) flow from Him, equipping us to live as holy and blameless representatives (Eph. 1:4). Like driftwood transformed by an artist's hand, we have no inherent value apart from Christ, but as His body, we are crafted into vessels of His glory, displaying His lordship to the world.

This dual role of Christ as head—leader and source— defines the church's mission as a Colony of Heaven. Roman colonists were chosen to represent their city's greatness, not to assimilate into foreign cultures but to transform their surroundings with Rome's values

(Levick, 1967). Similarly, the church is called to transform the world by reflecting Christ's kingdom, not conforming to worldly patterns (Rom. 12:2). When the world looks at us, they should see a community where Christ's authority is honored and His life-giving presence is evident—a colony where His love, truth, and grace shine forth, drawing others to the glory of our King.

Living as Heaven's Colony

Ephesians 1 is a call to embrace our identity as citizens of heaven's colony. Our salvation is not about our worthiness but about God's purpose to display His glory through us. We are chosen, adopted, redeemed, and sealed to reflect Christ's lordship, not to bask in our own significance. Every struggle we face, every habit God refines, every joy He grants is part of His plan to shape us into His image and proclaim His kingdom.

Consider again the driftwood analogy. To some, it's worthless, but to the artist, it's a canvas for beauty. God sees us not as we are but as He intends us to be —vessels of His glory. Our calling is to live in a way that points others to Christ, not to ourselves. As Paul prays for spiritual wisdom, let us seek the same, asking God to open our eyes to the hope, inheritance, and power He has given us.

As we journey through Ephesians, may we be drawn deeper into the sanctification God has designed for us. Let us pour our lives into displaying Christ, knowing that the same power that raised Him from the dead is at work in us. We are not waiting to "go home" to heaven; we are called to make heaven's reality visible here and now, as faithful citizens of God's eternal colony.

Prayer

Father, we are so thankful for the glorious hope You have given us in Christ. As we study Ephesians, draw us into the sanctification You have designed for us. May we pour our lives into displaying Christ, living as faithful citizens of Your kingdom. Open our eyes to see the greatness of our inheritance and the power at work in us, to the praise of Your glory. In Jesus' name,

Amen.

References:

Boardman, J. (1980). *The Greeks Overseas*. Thames & Hudson.

Bruce, F. F. (1984). *The Epistles to the Colossians, to Philemon, and to the Ephesians*. Eerdmans.

Clement of Alexandria. (1994). Stromata. In A. Roberts & J. Donaldson (Eds.), *The Ante-Nicene Fathers* (Vol. 2). Hendrickson. (Original work published ca. 200 A.D.)

Eusebius. (1885). *Church History*. In P. Schaff & H. Wace (Eds.), *Nicene and Post-Nicene Fathers* (Vol. 1). Christian Literature Publishing. (Original work published ca. 325 A.D.)

Graham, A. J. (1983). *Colony and Mother City in Ancient Greece*. Manchester University Press.

Hoehner, H. W. (2002). *Ephesians: An Exegetical Commentary*. Baker Academic.

Levick, B. (1967). *Roman Colonies in Southern Asia Minor*. Oxford University Press.

Metzger, B. M. (1994). *A Textual Commentary on the Greek New Testament*. United Bible Societies.

O'Brien, P. T. (1999). *The Letter to the Ephesians*. Eerdmans.

Salmon, E. T. (1969). *Roman Colonization Under the Republic*. Thames & Hudson.

Sherwin-White, A. N. (1963). *Roman Society and Roman Law in the New Testament*. Oxford University Press.

2

Walking Dead or Living Display

L ast chapter, we began our journey through Ephesians, marveling at the grandeur of God's plan in Chapter 1. We saw that believers are predestined in Christ to be a display on earth of what heaven will look like—a Colony of Heaven. As I reflected after I preached this sermon, I shared a thought on social media: the church is like a terrarium, a miniature model of the universe under Christ's rule. This idea shines brightly in Ephesians 1:22–23: "And hath put all things under his feet, and gave him to be the head over all things to the church, which is his body, the fulness of him that filleth all in all" (KJV). Christ, as head—both leader and source—directs and sustains the church, making it a showpiece of His sovereign reign. Our responsibility as His body is to reflect His authority and life, demonstrating to the world what creation will look like when fully surrendered to Him.

Ephesians 2:1–10 shifts focus from the cosmic plan to our personal transformation. Paul reminds us of our past as the "walking dead" and our new identity as a "living display" of God's grace. As citizens of heaven's colony, we are called not to drift with the world's current but to walk in the good works God has prepared, showcasing His kingdom in every aspect of our lives. This chapter challenges us: Are we living as the walking dead, driven by fleshly desires, or as a living display of Christ's transformative grace?

> *"And you hath he quickened, who were dead in trespasses and sins; Wherein in time past ye walked according to the course of this world, according to the prince of the power of the air, the spirit that now worketh in the children of disobedience: Among whom also we all had our conversation in times past in the lusts of our flesh, fulfilling the desires of the flesh and of the mind; and were by nature the children of wrath, even as others. But God, who is rich in mercy, for his great love wherewith he loved us, Even when we were dead in sins, hath quickened us together with Christ, (by grace ye are saved;) And hath raised us up together, and made us sit together in heavenly places in Christ Jesus: That in the ages to come he might shew the exceeding riches of his grace in his kindness toward us through Christ Jesus. For by grace are ye saved through faith; and that not of yourselves: it is the gift of God: Not of works, lest any man should boast. For we are his workmanship, created in Christ Jesus unto*

good works, which God hath before ordained that we should walk in them" (Eph. 2:1–10, KJV).

From Death to Life: Our Past and God's Mercy

Paul begins with a sobering reminder: "And you hath he quickened, who were dead in trespasses and sins" (Eph. 2:1, KJV). Before Christ, we were not merely struggling or misguided—we were dead. The phrase "walking dead" captures this paradox: we were alive in body but spiritually lifeless, driven by "trespasses and sins" (violations of God's boundaries and failures to meet His standards). I love the illustration of frog legs on a plate. Skinned and lifeless, they twitch and jump when sprinkled with salt, reacting to chemicals but devoid of true life. That's what life outside Christ is like—mere chemical reactions, chasing dopamine hits or fleshly cravings, whether pleasure, success, or self-fulfillment. It looks alive, but it's purposeless, a life of death.

Paul elaborates: "Wherein in time past ye walked according to the course of this world, according to the prince of the power of the air, the spirit that now worketh in the children of disobedience" (Eph. 2:2, KJV). The "course of this world" (Greek: *aiōn*, meaning the age or spirit of the times) is like a current sweeping us along. Young people today strive to be unique—different fashions, haircuts, slang—but ironically, they're all different in the same way, caught in the world's flow. This current is shaped by "the prince of the power of the air," Satan, who sets the atmosphere of selfishness and self-gratification. From movies to music, the world's message is clear: "Be true to yourself; get what you want." But as Paul warns elsewhere, "in me (that is, in my flesh,) dwelleth no good thing" (Rom. 7:18, KJV). Being "true to myself" without Christ leads to destruction, not life.

Verse 3 drives this home: "Among whom also we all had our conversation in times past in the lusts of our flesh, fulfilling the desires of the flesh and of the mind; and were by nature the children of wrath, even as others" (Eph. 2:3, KJV). Before Christ, we were all swept along, living for fleeting desires, our lives devoid of eternal purpose. Western philosophers like

> **Conversation**
>
> *Conversation* means "way of life" or "conduct".

Nietzsche, Hume, and Sartre, who embraced a self-focused, purposeless existence, often ended in despair, some even taking their own lives (Russell, 1945). Why? Because we were not created for a life of death but for God's glory.

Then come two glorious words: "But God" (Eph. 2:4, KJV). Despite our deadness, "God, who is rich in mercy, for his great love wherewith he loved us" intervened (Eph. 2:4, KJV). His mercy is boundless, never running out, available to all who receive it. Paul, who called himself the "chief" of sinners (1 Tim. 1:15, KJV), knew this mercy firsthand—a murderer of Christians transformed into Christ's apostle. God's love is not drawn to our loveliness; we had none. Instead, He *chose* to love us, transforming us into the image of His beloved Son, "who was with God" from eternity (John 1:1–2, KJV). Like driftwood—worthless to some, but a masterpiece in an artist's hands—God reshapes us to reflect Christ's likeness (O'Brien, 1999).

Made Alive in Christ

Paul declares, "Even when we were dead in sins, hath quickened us together with Christ, (by grace ye are saved;)" (Eph. 2:5, KJV). A dead thing cannot bring itself to life; life must come from outside. God, through Christ's resurrection, imparts His eternal life to us—the same life over which death has no power. This is not mere existence but a life of purpose, value, and meaning, flowing from our union with Christ, the head and source of His body (Eph. 1:22–23). As citizens of heaven's colony, we are no longer twitching frog legs, driven by chemical impulses, but living displays of Christ's resurrection power.

Paul continues, "And hath raised us up together, and made us sit together in heavenly places in Christ Jesus" (Eph. 2:6, KJV). This is a stunning reality: in Christ, we are already seated in heaven. Though we live on earth, our position in Christ places us under God's favor, judged as if we were with Christ at the Father's right hand. Why? "That in the ages to come he might shew the exceeding riches of his grace in his kindness toward us through Christ Jesus" (Eph. 2:7, KJV). We are God's eternal showpiece, a terrarium displaying His grace not only on earth but for all eternity, ruling with Christ as His bride (Rev. 21:2). Like a Roman colony showcasing the glory of Rome, the church reflects the immeasurable riches of God's kindness, transforming the world around us (Levick, 1967).

Saved by Grace Through Faith

Paul crystallizes this truth: "For by grace are ye saved through faith; and that not of yourselves: it is the gift ofGod: Not of works, lest any man should boast" (Eph. 2:8–9, KJV). Salvation is by grace—undeserved favor—through faith, which itself is God's gift. Faith is not mere intellectual assent but surrender, confessing "Jesus is Lord" and believing in His resurrection (Rom. 10:9, KJV). In America, we struggle to grasp what it means to call Jesus "Lord" because we've never lived under lords as they did in ancient or medieval times. In those days, a lord was far more than a title; he held absolute authority over his people's lives. Your lord determined where you could live—whether on his land or in a specific village. He decided your vocation, assigning you as a farmer, blacksmith, or servant. He even had a say in who you could marry, ensuring alliances or social order. Yet, the lord also provided for his people, supplying seed for planting, land to work, and protection from enemies (Le Goff, 1988). To call someone "Lord" was to submit to their authority in every aspect of life while trusting their provision and care.

When we confess "Jesus is Lord," we surrender our entire lives to His authority, just as citizens of a Roman colony submitted to Rome's rule to reflect its glory (Boardman, 1980). Christ, as our Lord, directs our path—where we live, how we work, how we relate to others—because He is the head of His body, both leading and sustaining us (Eph. 1:22–23, KJV). But unlike earthly lords, who could be harsh or self-serving, Jesus is the source of life, love, and grace, providing us with His Spirit and every spiritual blessing to fulfill His calling (Eph.1:3). To confess Him as Lord is to trust that His authority is good, His plans are perfect, and His provision is sufficient. You can say you believe Jesus is Lord, but if you haven't surrendered your will to Him—placing your life under His authority—there's no faith there. Faith is surrender, trusting who He is and what He promises. By His grace, God enables us to believe, offering faith as His gift, which we exercise by submitting to Christ's lordship (O'Brien, 1999).

This grace frees us from boasting. If salvation were by works, we could claim credit, but as Paul emphasizes, it's "not of yourselves." Like colonists chosen not for their inherent worth but for their city's purpose, we are saved to display God's glory, not ours. As citizens of heaven's colony, our faith in Christ's lordship empowers us to live under His rule, reflecting His kingdom in a world that follows "the prince of the power of the air" (Eph. 2:2, KJV).

His Workmanship for Good Works

Paul concludes, "For we are his workmanship, created in Christ Jesus unto good works, which God hath before ordained that we should walk in them" (Eph. 2:10, KJV). The word "workmanship" (Greek: *poiēma*, meaning masterpiece) paints a vivid picture. Imagine a pottery store displaying its finest piece in the window to showcase the artisan's skill. God places us, His masterpieces, on display to show what His grace can do. It's as though the purpose of my life is for God to say, "See what I can make out of James Burke? There's not much there, but look what My grace can do." We are His display piece, revealing what life looks like when centered on Christ.

These good works are not to earn salvation but to express it. God has prepared them "before ordained," tailoring them to our unique experiences, struggles, and gifts. Your life—your challenges overcome, lessons learned, and opportunities faced—is designed by God for specific works that I cannot do. Whether standing in line at the grocery store, navigating workplace conflicts, or guiding your family, God has placed you there to make choices that reflect Christ. This perspective transforms daily life. Instead of taking the path of least resistance, we ask, "How would God's workmanship behave in this moment?" As citizens of heaven's colony, our actions should radiate Christ's love, truth, and grace, transforming our surroundings as a colony transforms its region (Graham, 1983).

Living as a Display of Grace

Ephesians 2:1–10 challenges us to examine our walk: Are we the walking dead, driven by the world's current and fleshly desires, or a living display of God's grace? As citizens of heaven's colony, we are called to reflect Christ, our head, who leads and sustains us. Just as Roman colonists were chosen to represent their city's glory, we are God's workmanship, created to display His kingdom through good works prepared for us. This is not about earning His favor but about living out the life He has given us—a life of purpose, powered by His resurrection power and sustained by His boundless mercy.

Consider the frog legs again: twitching but lifeless, reacting to the world's impulses. Now contrast that with the terrarium—a vibrant, purposeful display of life under Christ's rule. That's our calling: to live differently, with eternal priorities, laying up treasures in heaven (Matt. 6:20). Every interaction, every decision, is an opportunity to show the world what life looks like when surrendered to Christ. As His body, filled by Him who "filleth all in all" (Eph. 1:23, KJV), we are empowered to walk in His works, making His kingdom visible here and now.

Closing Challenge

Are you walking dead, or are you a living display? Have you surrendered to Jesus Christ, placing your faith in Him as Lord? If you are a living display, are you walking in the good works God has prepared for you? As citizens of heaven's colony, let us live as His masterpiece, reflecting His grace in every circumstance.

Prayer

Father, we pray that our hearts will be surrendered to You completely. Lord, in every situation and circumstance, help us remember not to be guided by the desires of our flesh but to recognize that our steps are ordered by You. May we see the works You have designed for us and walk in them, displaying Your grace to the world and for eternity. In Jesus' name we pray,

Amen.

References:

Boardman, J. (1980). *The Greeks Overseas*. Thames & Hudson.

Cohen-Solal, A. (1987). *Sartre: A Life*. Pantheon Books.

Graham, A. J. (1983). *Colony and Mother City in Ancient Greece*. Manchester University Press.

Kaufmann, W. (1974). *Nietzsche: Philosopher, Psychologist, Antichrist*. Princeton University Press.

Le Goff, J. (1988). *Medieval Civilization: 400–1500*. Blackwell Publishing.

Levick, B. (1967). *Roman Colonies in Southern Asia Minor*. Oxford University Press.

Mossner, E. C. (1980). *The Life of David Hume*. Oxford University Press.

O'Brien, P. T. (1999). *The Letter to the Ephesians*. Eerdmans.

Russell, B. (1945). *A History of Western Philosophy*. Simon & Schuster.

3

The Church: God's Cosmic Display

In our journey through Ephesians, we've seen the church's high calling as a Colony of Heaven. Chapter 1 revealed our predestination in Christ to display His lordship, like a terrarium showcasing the universe under His rule (Eph. 1:22–23, KJV). Chapter 2 transformed us from "walking dead" to a "living display" of God's grace, surrendered to Christ's lordship (Eph. 2:1–10, KJV). Now, Ephesians 2:11–3:21 unveils the church's cosmic purpose: to display God's multifaceted wisdom to heavenly

Terrarium

A small enclosed container displaying soil, plants, and miniature ecosystem.

beings (Eph. 3:10). We often think life is about our satisfaction, but as the story of Lazarus and the rich man shows, true purpose lies in glorifying God (Luke 16:19–31, KJV). Lazarus, lying in the gutter with dogs licking his sores, wasn't satisfied in an earthly sense, yet God loved him. For 2,000 years, his story has glorified God, and he wouldn't trade places with the rich man for anything. So, what is the church? Why do we gather? Ephesians reveals a purpose far beyond fellowship or personal growth—a divine mission to show the universe who God is.

"Wherefore remember, that ye being in time past Gentiles in the flesh, who are called Uncircumcision by that which is called the Circumcision in the flesh made by hands; That at that time ye were without Christ, being aliens from the commonwealth of Israel, and strangers from the covenants of promise, having no hope, and without God in the world: But now in Christ Jesus ye who sometimes were far off are made nigh by the blood of Christ. For he is our peace, who hath made both one, and hath broken down the middle wall of partition between us; Having abolished in his flesh the enmity, even the law of commandments contained in ordinances; for to make in himself of twain one new man, so making peace; And that he might reconcile both unto God in one body by the cross, having slain the enmity thereby: And came and preached peace to you which were afar off, and to them that were nigh. For through him we both have access by one Spirit unto the Father. Now therefore ye are no more strangers and foreigners, but fellow citizens with the saints, and of the household of God; And are built upon the foundation of the apostles and prophets, Jesus Christ himself

being the chief corner stone; In whom all the building fitly framed together groweth unto an holy temple in the Lord: In whom ye also are builded together for an habitation of God through the Spirit. For this cause I Paul, the prisoner of Jesus Christ for you Gentiles, If ye have heard of the dispensation of the grace of God which is given me to you-ward: How that by revelation he made known unto me the mystery; (as I wrote afore in few words, Whereby, when ye read, ye may understand my knowledge in the mystery of Christ) Which in other ages was not made known unto the sons of men, as it is now revealed unto his holy apostles and prophets by the Spirit; That the Gentiles should be fellowheirs, and of the same body, and partakers of his promise in Christ by the gospel: Whereof I was made a minister, according to the gift of the grace of God given unto me by the effectual working of his power. Unto me, who am less than the least of all saints, is this grace given, that I should preach among the Gentiles the unsearchable riches of Christ; And to make all men see what is the fellowship of the mystery, which from the beginning of the world hath been hid in God, who created all things by Jesus Christ: To the intent that now unto the principalities and powers in heavenly places might be known by the church the manifold wisdom of God,

According to the eternal purpose which he purposed in Christ Jesus our Lord: In whom we have boldness and access with confidence by the faith of him. Wherefore I desire that ye faint not at my tribulations for you, which is your glory. For this cause I bow my knees unto the Father of our Lord Jesus Christ, Of whom the whole family in heaven and earth is named, That he would grant you, according to the riches of his glory, to be strengthened with might by his Spirit in the inner man; That Christ may dwell in your hearts by faith; that ye, being rooted and grounded in love, May be able to comprehend with all saints what is the breadth, and length, and depth, and height; And to know the love of Christ, which passeth knowledge, that ye might be filled with all the fulness of God. Now unto him that is able to do exceeding abundantly above all that we ask or think, according to the power that worketh in us, Unto him be glory in the church by Christ Jesus throughout all ages, world without end. Amen" (Eph. 2:11–3:21, KJV).

Strangers and Aliens (Ephesians 2:11–12)

Paul begins, "Wherefore remember, that ye being in time past Gentiles in the flesh... were without Christ, being aliens from the commonwealth of Israel, and strangers from the covenants of promise, having no hope, and without God in the world" (Eph. 2:11–12, KJV). Before Christ, Gentiles were spiritual outsiders —excluded from Israel's covenants, without access to the temple's inner courts, and devoid of hope. Like foreigners barred from a Roman colony's privileges, Gentiles had no claim to God's promises (O'Brien, 1999). This separation wasn't just social; it was spiritual, leaving them under the world's current, driven by "the prince of the power of the air" (Eph. 2:2, KJV). Yet, this bleak past sets the stage for God's redemptive plan, showing the church's purpose as a unified display of His grace.

Christ Our Peace (Ephesians 2:13–18)

"But now in Christ Jesus ye who sometimes were far off are made nigh by the blood of Christ. For he is our peace" (Eph. 2:13–14, KJV). Christ's death shattered the "middle wall of partition," the hostility between Jew and Gentile rooted in the law's ordinances. In Solomon's temple, a literal wall separated the Court of the Gentiles from the inner courts, symbolizing exclusion (1 Kings 8:41–43). Jesus, by His sacrifice, tore down this barrier, just as He rent the temple veil (Matt. 27:51, KJV), granting access to God for all. He created "one new man" (Eph. 2:15, KJV), reconciling both groups into one body through the cross.

Imagine two rival towns, divided by a river and years of conflict, each with its own customs and pride. A wise leader builds a bridge, unites the towns into one city, and establishes a shared identity under his rule. So Christ, our peace, unites Jew and Gentile into one Colony of Heaven, where His lordship—His authority and provision (Eph. 2:8–9)—defines our life together (Le Goff, 1988). Through Him, "we both have access by one Spirit unto the Father" (Eph. 2:18, KJV), a privilege that reveals God's love to heavenly beings watching in awe (Eph. 3:10).

Citizens and Temple (Ephesians 2:19–22)

"Now therefore ye are no more strangers and foreigners, but fellowcitizens with the saints, and of the household of God" (Eph. 2:19, KJV). Paul uses citizenship imagery, familiar to his Roman audience. Roman colonies, like Philippi, were outposts of Rome's culture, where citizens—regardless of birthplace—lived to display Roman values in foreign lands (Levick, 1967). They didn't aim to return to Rome but to make Rome visible where they were. Similarly, we are citizens of heaven's colony, not waiting to escape earth but called to show heaven's culture—love, peace, and holiness—here and now. As God's household, we are family, united under Christ's lordship, reflecting His glory as Lazarus did, not for our satisfaction but for God's eternal purpose (Luke 16:19–31).

The church is also "built upon the foundation of the apostles and prophets, Jesus Christ himself being the chief corner stone" (Eph. 2:20, KJV). The cornerstone aligns the building, bearing its weight and uniting its walls. The apostles (New Testament) and prophets (Old Testament) form the foundation, but without Christ, they don't hold together. Rejecting either testament, as some do, is like tearing down half the house. In Christ, "all the building fitly framed together groweth unto an holy temple in the Lord" (Eph. 2:21, KJV), a dwelling place for God's Spirit. Individually, we are temples of the Holy Spirit (1Cor. 6:19); corporately, our gatherings in places like your church are where God meets His people, not because the room is holy but because we, His redeemed, are holy.

God's Cosmic Display (Ephesians 3:1–21)

Paul transitions to his role: "For this cause I Paul, the prisoner of Jesus Christ for you Gentiles" (Eph. 3:1, KJV). His imprisonment, far from a setback, is for the Gentiles' glory, revealing the "mystery" that they are "fellowheirs, and of the same body" with believing Jews (Eph. 3:6, KJV). This mystery, hidden for ages, is the church—God's masterpiece, displaying His wisdom to "principalities and powers in heavenly places" (Eph. 3:10, KJV).

Heavenly beings, who sang at creation (Job 38:7), have watched God's works—from galaxies arranged like lacework to His dealings with humanity. Yet, only through the church do they see facets of God's character: His grace in uniting diverse peoples, His

> **Mystery**
>
> *In the New Testament, a mystery is a truth that has not been revealed before, but is being made known now.*

love in Christ's sacrifice, and His power in our new life (O'Brien, 1999).

This cosmic display is not about us at the center. When we gather to worship, pray, share burdens, or partake in ordinances, we show angels who God is. Imagine a small art gallery displaying a masterpiece to a cosmic audience. Our unity in Christ—lifting His name wherever you are, alongside churches worldwide—reveals God's manifold wisdom. As Paul says, "Unto him be glory in the church by Christ Jesus throughout all ages, world without end" (Eph. 3:21, KJV). Our suffering, like Paul's, is reframed as a privilege when seen in this eternal context (Eph. 3:13).

Paul's prayer in Ephesians 3:14–19 is a plea for us to grasp this calling: to be strengthened by the Spirit, to have Christ dwell in our hearts, and to comprehend the vast love of Christ, "that ye might be filled with all the fulness of God" (Eph. 3:19, KJV). Like a colony reflecting its home city's glory, we are filled by Christ, our head, to display His kingdom to the universe (Eph. 1:22–23).

Living as God's Masterpiece

Ephesians 2:11–3:21 challenges us to see the church's true purpose: not our satisfaction, but God's glory. We are not merely a community for fellowship or support, but a Colony of Heaven, united in Christ to display His wisdom to heavenly realms. Every act of worship, every prayer for one another, every step of obedience is a brushstroke in God's masterpiece, revealing His character to angels and humanity alike. Like Lazarus, our lives—however humble or afflicted—glorify God when surrendered to His purpose (Luke 16:19–31, KJV). As citizens of His kingdom, we are called to live in unity, reflecting the peace Christ established on the cross and the love that surpasses knowledge.

Recall the divided city we envisioned, its neighborhoods split by rivalry until a visionary leader built bridges to unite them under one rule. So Christ, our cornerstone, has reconciled us—Jew and Gentile, your city and beyond—into one body, His holy temple (Eph. 2:14–16, 21, KJV). Our gatherings, whether in a small church or across the globe, make God's presence visible, showing the world and the heavens what life looks like under His lordship. Let us not say, "I can worship God in the woods as well as in church," for the church's purpose transcends personal devotion—it is God's cosmic display, revealing His glory through our unity and obedience.

Closing Challenge

Are you living as a citizen of heaven's colony, united with others to display God's glory? Have you surrendered to Christ's lordship, trusting His peace to guide your relationships? As God's masterpiece, let us commit to worship, pray, and serve together, showing the world and the heavens who our God is. Let our lives, like Lazarus's, glorify Him for eternity.

Prayer

Father, we bow before You, the Father of every family in heaven and earth. Strengthen us by Your Spirit to live as Your holy temple, united in Christ. Help us comprehend the vastness of Your love and be filled with Your fulness, that we may display Your wisdom to all creation. May our worship, prayers, and actions glorify You forever. Unto You be glory in the church by Christ Jesus, world without end. In His name we pray,

Amen.

References:

Boardman, J. (1980). *The Greeks Overseas*. Thames & Hudson.

Graham, A. J. (1983). *Colony and Mother City in Ancient Greece*. Manchester University Press.

Le Goff, J. (1988). *Medieval Civilization: 400–1500*. Blackwell Publishing.

Levick, B. (1967). *Roman Colonies in Southern Asia Minor*. Oxford University Press.

O'Brien, P. T. (1999). *The Letter to the Ephesians*. Eerdmans.

4

Walk Worthy of Our Calling

Through Ephesians, we've seen the church as a Colony of Heaven, called to display God's glory. In Chapter 1, we marveled at our predestination in Christ to reflect His lordship, like a terrarium showcasing His kingdom (Eph. 1:4–14, 22–23, KJV). Chapter 2 transformed us from "walking dead" to a "living display" of His grace, surrendered to His authority (Eph. 2:1–10). Chapter 3 unveiled the church's cosmic purpose, uniting Jew and Gentile to reveal God's wisdom to heavenly beings (Eph. 3:10, KJV). Now, in Ephesians 4:1–16, Paul urges us to "walk worthy" of this calling, living as one body under Christ's headship. The church is not just a gathering for fellowship but a masterpiece displaying Christ's character on earth and in heaven. How do we walk together in a way that reflects our high calling? Let's explore Paul's practical charge to live in unity and maturity as God's Colony of Heaven.

> *"I therefore, the prisoner of the Lord, beseech you that ye walk worthy of the vocation wherewith ye are called, With all lowliness and meekness, with longsuffering, forbearing one another in love; Endeavouring to keep the unity*

of the Spirit in the bond of peace. There is one body, and one Spirit, even as ye are called in one hope of your calling; One Lord, one faith, one baptism, One God and Father of all, who is above all, and through all, and in you all. But unto every one of us is given grace according to the measure of the gift of Christ. Wherefore he saith, When he ascended up on high, he led captivity captive, and gave gifts unto men. (Now that he ascended, what is it but that he also descended first into the lower parts of the earth? He that descended is the same also that ascended up far above all heavens, that he might fill all things.) And he gave some, apostles; and some, prophets; and some, evangelists; and some, pastors and teachers; For the perfecting of the saints, for the work of the ministry, for the edifying of the body of Christ: Till we all come in the unity of the faith, and of the knowledge of the Son of God, unto a perfect man, unto the measure of the stature of the fulness of Christ: That we henceforth be no more children, tossed to and fro, and carried about with every wind of doctrine, by the sleight of men, and cunning craftiness, whereby they lie in wait to deceive; But speaking the truth in love, may grow up into him in all things, which is the head, even Christ: From whom the whole body fitly joined together and compacted by that which every joint supplieth, according to the effectual working in the measure of every part, maketh increase of the body unto the edifying of itself in love" (Eph. 4:1–16, KJV).

Called to Walk Worthy (Ephesians 4:1–6)

Paul begins, "I therefore, the prisoner of the Lord, beseech you that ye walk worthy of the vocation wherewith ye are called" (Eph. 4:1, KJV). As in Chapter 3, he identifies as "the prisoner of the Lord," chained in Rome for preaching the gospel, under house arrest yet proclaiming Christ to all who visit (Acts 28:30–31, KJV). His imprisonment doesn't diminish his authority but underscores his commitment to our calling as a Colony of Heaven—a terrarium displaying Christ's lordship on earth and in heaven (Eph. 1:22–23; 3:10). This calling, explored in Chapters 1–3, is to be God's masterpiece, showing His grace and wisdom (O'Brien, 1999). To "walk worthy" means living daily—our thoughts, interactions, priorities—in a way that reflects this high purpose.

Walking worthy requires discipline, like medical doctors or military special forces who train rigorously for their roles. Do we want to live like the world, chasing fleeting desires only to end life with little meaning? Or will we, as Hebrews urges, "lay aside every weight, and the sin which doth so easily beset us, and… run with patience the race that is set before us" (Heb. 12:1, KJV)?

This isn't an individual stroll but a collective march. We're called together as one body, walking in step with "all lowliness and meekness, with longsuffering, forbearing one another in love" (Eph. 4:2, KJV). Humility acknowledges every member's necessity; gentleness cares for each other's feelings; patience bears with one another in love. We make "every effort to keep the unity of the Spirit in the bond of peace" (Eph. 4:3, KJV), maintaining the unity Christ forged (Ch. 3; Eph. 2:14).

Paul grounds this unity in eternal truths: "There is one body, and one Spirit, even as ye are called in one hope of your calling; One Lord, one faith, one baptism, One God and Father of all" (Eph. 4:4–6, KJV). In Paul's day, each city had one church, unlike today's many denominations. I love the story of the man on a desert island with three huts: "This is where I live, that's where I go to church, and that's where I used to go but I quit." Yet, there's only one body of Christ. Leaving a church over disagreements doesn't escape the body—it abandons your assignment within it. This one body is energized by one Spirit, driven not by worldly priorities but by pleasing Christ, our head (Ch. 1). We share one hope—eternal life with Jesus ruling at His side (Eph. 1:18). One Lord, Jesus Christ, calls the shots through His Word (Ch. 2). One faith, one baptism, one God unites us as a Colony of Heaven, displaying His kingdom in a divided world (Levick, 1967).

Gifts and Responsibilities (Ephesians 4:7–12)

"But unto every one of us is given grace according to the measure of the gift of Christ" (Eph. 4:7, KJV). Christ, having "ascended up on high," fulfilled Psalm 68:18, leading "captivity captive" and giving gifts to His people (Eph. 4:8, KJV). Unlike a conquering king receiving tribute, Christ **gives** gifts—responsibilities to maintain order in His kingdom. He "descended first into the lower parts of the earth" and "ascended up far above all heavens, that he might fill all things" (Eph. 4:9–10, KJV). Through us, His body, Christ remains on earth as His ambassadors, displaying His presence (Ch. 3).

These gifts include "some, apostles; and some, prophets; and some, evangelists; and some, pastors and teachers" (Eph. 4:11, KJV). Apostles and prophets laid the foundation (Eph. 2:20); today, prophets proclaim the written Word, evangelists spread the gospel, and pastors and teachers shepherd and feed the flock. Their purpose is "for the perfecting of the saints, for the work of the ministry, for the edifying of the body of Christ" (Eph. 4:12, KJV). Too often, churches think they're hiring a pastor to do all the ministry—preaching, visiting, praying—as if he's a hired hand to carry the load. But Paul makes it clear: the pastor is Christ's gift to the church, not to do the work alone but to equip the saints for the work of ministry. Like a coach training players, not playing the game himself, the pastor prepares the congregation to serve, teach, and build up the body (O'Brien, 1999). Every believer has a role—whether teaching a class, serving a meal, praying for the hurting, or sharing the gospel. In a Colony of Heaven, each citizen contributes to the community's mission, just as Roman colonists worked together to reflect their city's glory (Boardman, 1980). When we expect the pastor to do everything, we rob the body of its purpose and hinder the display of Christ's lordship (Ch. 2).

Growing into Maturity (Ephesians 4:13–16)

The goal is clear: "Till we all come in the unity of the faith, and of the knowledge of the Son of God, unto a perfect man, unto the measure of the stature of the fulness of Christ" (Eph. 4:13, KJV). The church must grow into Christ's likeness, unified and mature. We must stop being "children, tossed to and fro, and carried about with every wind of doctrine" (Eph. 4:14, KJV), swayed by deceitful schemes. Maturity means stability, rooted in Christ, our head.

How? By "speaking the truth in love" (Eph. 4:15, KJV), or as we might put it, "practicing the truth in love." Truth without love becomes a cudgel; love without truth becomes sentimental permissiveness. Practicing truth means living it—forgiving when we know we should, pursuing purity by setting aside distractions. You can know you need to forgive, but until you do, it doesn't change you. Once you practice love, you become more loving. Through this, we "grow up into him in all things, which is the head, even Christ" (Eph. 4:15, KJV).

Picture a caricature: a huge head with a tiny body. That's us—Christ is the head, but our body, the church, must grow to carry Him properly. "From whom the whole body fitly joined together and compacted by that which every joint supplieth maketh increase of the body unto the edifying of itself in love" (Eph. 4:16, KJV). The life flows from Christ, but the strength comes from our unity, as each part does its work. Like a Roman colony growing into a thriving city, the church builds itself up in love, displaying Christ's fullness to the world and heavens (Ch. 3; Graham, 1983).

Living Worthy of the Calling

Ephesians 4:1–16 calls us to walk worthy as a Colony of Heaven, united in the Spirit and growing into Christ's likeness. We're not on an individual stroll but marching together, with humility, gentleness, and patience. Like the man on the desert island, we can't quit the body—every member is vital. Christ equips us with gifts, like a coach training players, to build His church. By practicing truth in love, we grow from childish instability to maturity, reflecting the stature of our head, Christ. Our gatherings in our local church or beyond are not about personal satisfaction but about displaying God's glory, as Lazarus did (Ch. 3), through our unified walk.

Closing Challenge

Are you walking worthy of your calling, living in humility to maintain the Spirit's unity? Are you practicing truth in love, using Christ's gifts to build His body? As God's Colony of Heaven, let us commit to serving together, growing into maturity, and reflecting Christ's fullness in all we do.

Prayer

Father, make us a church that represents You well in this place. May each of us do our part, practicing truth in love, growing into maturity, building the body up in love. In Jesus' name we pray,

Amen.

References:

Boardman, J. (1980). *The Greeks Overseas.* Thames & Hudson.

Graham, A. J. (1983). *Colony and Mother City in Ancient Greece.* Manchester University Press.

Le Goff, J. (1988). *Medieval Civilization: 400–1500.* Blackwell Publishing.

Levick, B. (1967). *Roman Colonies in Southern Asia Minor.* Oxford University Press.

O'Brien, P. T. (1999). *The Letter to the Ephesians.* Eerdmans.

5

Put Off the Old, Put On the New

Our journey through Ephesians has revealed the church's high calling as a Colony of Heaven—an outpost of God's kingdom displaying His glory to earth and the heavens. In Chapter 1, we marveled at our predestination in Christ to reflect His lordship, like a terrarium showcasing His eternal plan (Eph. 1:4–14, 22–23, KJV). Chapter 2 transformed us from "walking dead" to a "living display" of His grace, surrendered to His authority (Eph. 2:1–10). Chapter 3 unveiled the church's cosmic purpose, uniting Jew and Gentile to reveal God's manifold wisdom to heavenly beings (Eph. 3:10). Chapter 4 called us to "walk worthy" of this vocation, living in unity as one body under Christ's headship (Eph. 4:1–16). Now, in Ephesians 4:17–32, Paul turns to the individual believer within that body, urging us to live transformed lives as citizens of heaven's colony. We are not to walk as the world does, in futile rebellion, but to put off the old man, be renewed in our minds, and put on the new man created in Christ's image. This chapter challenges us: Are we clinging to the corrupt ways of the old man, or are we reflecting the righteousness and holiness of our King? Let us heed Paul's call to live distinctly, strengthening the body and displaying God's glory.

"This I say therefore, and testify in the Lord, that ye henceforth walk not as other Gentiles walk, in the vanity of their mind, Having the understanding darkened, being alienated from the life of God through the ignorance that is in them, because of the blindness of their heart: Who being past feeling have given themselves over unto lasciviousness, to work all uncleanness with greediness. But ye have not so learned Christ; If so be that ye have heard him, and have been taught by him, as the truth is in Jesus: That ye put off concerning the former conversation the old man, which is corrupt according to the deceitful lusts; And be renewed in the spirit of your mind; And that ye put on the new man, which after God is created in righteousness and true holiness. Wherefore putting away lying, speak every man truth with his neighbour: for we are members one of another. Be ye angry, and sin not: let not the sun go down upon your wrath: Neither give place to the devil. Let him that stole steal no more: but rather let him labour, working with his hands the thing which is good, that he may have to give to him that needeth. Let no corrupt communication proceed out of your mouth, but that which is good to the use of edifying, that it

may minister grace unto the hearers. And grieve not the holy Spirit of God, whereby ye are sealed unto the day of redemption. Let all bitterness, and wrath, and anger, and clamour, and evil speaking, be put away from you, with all malice: And be ye kind one to another, tenderhearted, forgiving one another, even as God for Christ's sake hath forgiven you."
Ephesians 4:17–32 (KJV)

The Old Man's Futile Life (Ephesians 4:17–19)

Paul begins with a solemn charge: "This I say therefore, and testify in the Lord, that ye henceforth walk not as other Gentiles walk, in the vanity of their mind" (Eph. 4:17, KJV). As a prisoner for the gospel, Paul speaks with authority, not offering a suggestion but a command rooted in Christ's lordship (Eph. 4:1; O'Brien, 1999). The Gentiles—those outside Christ—live in "vanity of their mind," a futile way of thinking that leads nowhere. Our minds are like a computer with "garbage in, garbage out." Without salvation, the mind lacks the grid of God's truth, and, having only the lies of the world to guide it, produces empty, purposeless actions. Paul elaborates: "Having the understanding darkened, being alienated from the life of God through the ignorance that is in them, because of the blindness of their heart" (Eph. 4:18, KJV). The Greek word for "blindness" here is *pōrōsis*, meaning a hardening or callousness, like a heart so toughened it no longer feels conviction (Hoehner, 2002). I've seen this in folks who say, "If I believe that, I'll have to change my life—so I won't." Their willful ignorance shuts out God's life, leaving them "past feeling" and plunging into "lasciviousness, to work all uncleanness with greediness" (Eph. 4:19, KJV). This is the old man's life—driven by deceitful desires, chasing pleasures that corrupt and destroy.

As citizens of heaven's colony, we are called to a different walk. Roman colonists in places like Philippi didn't adopt local barbarian customs; they shed them to embody Rome's culture, transforming their surroundings (Levick, 1967). Similarly, we must reject the world's futile ways. The old man's calloused heart has no place in God's colony, where we are to reflect Christ's righteousness and holiness, making His kingdom visible in our lives.

The New Man in Christ (Ephesians 4:20–24)

Paul contrasts this bleak picture with our calling: "But ye have not so learned Christ; If so be that ye have heard him, and have been taught by him, as the truth is in Jesus" (Eph. 4:20–21, KJV). Believers know better. The Spirit dwells in us, and the truth of Jesus exposes the lie of worldly living. When we live like the world, we do so against our new nature, grieving the Spirit who seals us (Eph. 4:30). Paul outlines a threefold process: "That ye put off concerning the former conversation the old man, which is corrupt according to the deceitful lusts; And be renewed in the spirit of your mind; And that ye put on the new man, which after God is created in righteousness and true holiness" (Eph. 4:22–24, KJV).

First, we must "put off" the old man—the sinful nature at home in this world, "dead in trespasses and sins" (Eph. 2:1, KJV). Its desires are deceitful, promising life but delivering death. The flesh craves endlessly, never satisfied, and its pursuits destroy us. If we eat to feel better, chasing comfort in food, our health suffers—obesity, disease, or addiction take hold. If we dull pain with substances, seeking escape in alcohol or drugs, we ravage our souls and bodies, trading fleeting relief for lasting ruin. If we pursue pleasure in sexual behavior outside God's design, it intensifies our loneliness, leaving us emptier than before. Every fleshly desire—whether for power, approval, or gratification—looks good, feels good, but kills us if left unchecked, pulling us deeper into the world's futile cycle (O'Brien, 1999). Putting off the old man is deliberate, like shedding filthy clothes, rejecting the lie that the flesh can ever be satisfied. Second, we are to "be renewed in the spirit of your mind." This isn't self-improvement but a transformation by God's Spirit, reshaping how we think to align with His truth (Rom. 12:2). Finally, we "put on the new man," created in God's image, reflecting His righteousness (treating others justly) and true holiness (a life set apart for His calling).

I love the illustration of a caterpillar becoming a butterfly—a divine masterpiece of transformation, painted by the Creator's hand. It doesn't merely sprout wings, as if adding a new feature to its old form. No, the caterpillar retreats into a silken cocoon, a hidden crucible where its very essence unravels. There, in the quiet darkness, it melts into a formless goo—its crawling, earthbound identity dissolved, surrendered to God's design. From this chaos, the Spirit of creation weaves a miracle: delicate wings, vibrant with colors that mirror heaven's glory, emerge where once was only a worm. A butterfly  takes flight, no longer bound to the dust but soaring in beauty, a living testament to the Artist's power (Bruce, 1984). So it is with us. In the garden, the Son formed Adam from dust, breathing into him the breath of life as God's image-bearer (Gen. 2:7). Adam fell, but in Christ, the second Adam, God stamps His image anew (1 Cor. 15:45–49). This transformation is no mere patching of our old nature; it is radical, from the inside out, as the Spirit re-creates us into vessels of righteousness and holiness. As citizens of heaven's colony, we don't chase the world's fleeting desires; we are too enthralled by heaven's work, soaring in the beauty of our King's design to display His kingdom's glory.

Practical Transformation (Ephesians 4:25–32)

Paul now applies this transformation to daily life: "Wherefore putting away lying, speak every man truth with his neighbour: for we are members one of another" (Eph. 4:25, KJV). Quoting Zechariah 8:16, Paul addresses a church where dishonesty crept in— a reminder that even God's people need this exhortation. Lying isn't just telling whoppers—bold, blatant falsehoods that deceive outright. It's also the subtler sins we slip into: making excuses to dodge accountability, like saying, "I didn't have time," when we chose not to prioritize; or failing to correct an error when we know the truth, letting a half-truth stand to save face; or misrepresenting our intentions to look better than we are. These small dishonesties erode trust, like cracks in the joints of a frame (Eph. 4:16, KJV). As citizens of heaven's colony, we are interconnected, each truth strengthening the body, each lie tearing at its unity. A Roman colony's strength lay in its fidelity to Rome's standards; any compromise weakened its witness (Levick, 1967). So it is with us—dishonesty, big or small, dishonors our King and dims His kingdom's glory.

Next, Paul says, "Be ye angry, and sin not: let not the sun go down upon your wrath: Neither give place to the devil" (Eph. 4:26–27, KJV). Anger isn't always sin —Jesus was angry (Mark 3:5)—but it must be handled quickly. Unresolved anger curdles into bitterness, giving the devil a "foothold" (Greek: *topos*), a place, a wedge to whisper discouragement and division (O'Brien, 1999). Sometimes you can't fix the issue; forgive and move on, trusting God's justice. As citizens of heaven's colony, we don't let anger fester, weakening the body's witness.

Paul adds, "Let him that stole steal no more: but rather let him labour, working with his hands the thing which is good, that he may have to give to him that needeth" (Eph. 4:28, KJV). Stealing—whether robbing banks or sponging off others, taking without contributing—has no place in God's colony. Instead, we are to work productively with our hands, creating something valuable that adds to society, like Paul stitching leather tents late into the night to support his ministry (Acts 18:3; 1 Cor. 4:12). His calloused hands were a testimony of selfless labor, not to amass wealth or hoard riches, but to have something to share with those in need (Bruce, 1984). In God's colony, we labor diligently—whether crafting goods, serving others, or building community—not to get rich, but to care for others, reflecting Christ's generosity that pours out for the body's good.

Our speech must also change: "Let no corrupt communication proceed out of your mouth, but that which is good to the use of edifying, that it may minister grace unto the hearers" (Eph. 4:29, KJV). "Corrupt" (Greek: *sapros*) means rotten, like spoiled fruit. Our words should be Spirit-infused, building up the body and giving grace, even when correction is needed. Harsh or careless words grieve "the holy Spirit of God, whereby ye are sealed unto the day of redemption" (Eph. 4:30, KJV). I believe this grieving especially concerns our speech within the body of the church, as it disrupts the Spirit's work of unity (Hoehner, 2002). As heaven's colonists, our words should reflect Christ's love, not the world's decay.

Finally, Paul commands, "Let all bitterness, and wrath, and anger, and clamour, and evil speaking, be put away from you, with all malice: And be ye kind one to another, tenderhearted, forgiving one another, even as God for Christ's sake hath forgiven you" (Eph. 4:31–32, KJV). Bitterness and malice are like poison, corroding the body's unity. Instead, we practice kindness, compassion, and forgiveness, mirroring God's forgiveness in Christ. That hurt you're carrying —Christ died for it. Someone has already suffered for that sin, you don't have to seek revenge. We can release vengeance to God, who judges justly (1 Pet. 2:23), and forgive, freeing ourselves to love as Christ loves.

Living as Heaven's Colony

Ephesians 4:17–32 challenges us to examine our walk: Are we clinging to the old man's futile ways, or are we living as the new man, reflecting Christ's image? As citizens of heaven's colony, our transformation strengthens the body's witness. Roman colonists didn't blend into local cultures; they transformed their surroundings by living out Rome's values (Boardman, 1980). Likewise, we shed the world's calloused heart (*pōrōsis*) and deceitful desires to display Christ's righteousness and holiness. Every choice—our words, anger, work, and forgiveness—either builds up the body or hinders its mission to show God's glory.

Consider again the caterpillar, melting into goo to become a butterfly. God doesn't patch up our old nature; He re-creates us in Christ, stamping His image anew. Or think of Paul, stitching leather to serve others, his hands calloused not from hardness of heart but from love for the body. Our lives should be like his—marked by selfless labor, truthful speech, and forgiving love, making heaven's culture visible in our homes, workplaces, and churches. When the world sees us, they should see a community where Christ reigns, not a mirror of their futile ways.

This transformation isn't solitary. God didn't call us to walk this world alone. He gave us a body—brothers and sisters to love and share this life with. Our individual choices impact the whole, like stones in a temple "fitly framed together" (Eph. 2:21). Lying, bitterness, or corrupt words weaken the body's witness; truth, kindness, and forgiveness strengthen it, displaying Christ to a watching world and heavenly beings (Eph. 3:10).

Closing Challenge

Are you living as the old man, driven by the world's "garbage in, garbage out" thinking, or as the new man, created in God's image? Have you put off lying, unresolved anger, or selfish habits? Are your words and actions building up the body, ministering grace? As citizens of heaven's colony, let us commit to shedding the old man's ways and putting on the new —living in righteousness and holiness to reflect our King. Let our lives, like Paul's leather-working hands, show selfless love, making Christ's kingdom visible here and now.

Prayer

Father, thank You that You did not call us to walk this world alone. You gave us a body, brothers and sisters to love and share this life with. Help us to put off the stinking old man— his lies, bitterness, and selfish ways. By the transforming power of Your Word and Spirit, renew our minds and form Your image in us, that we may love one another as Christ loved us. May our words, work, and forgiveness display Your glory, strengthening Your colony to shine in this world. In Jesus' name we pray, Amen.

References

Boardman, J. (1980). *The Greeks Overseas*. Thames & Hudson.

Bruce, F. F. (1984). *The Epistles to the Colossians, to Philemon, and to the Ephesians*. Eerdmans.

Graham, A. J. (1983). *Colony and Mother City in Ancient Greece*. Manchester University Press.

Hoehner, H. W. (2002). *Ephesians: An Exegetical Commentary*. Baker Academic.

Levick, B. (1967). *Roman Colonies in Southern Asia Minor*. Oxford University Press.

O'Brien, P. T. (1999). *The Letter to the Ephesians* Eerdmans.

6

Rules for Relationships

Our journey through Ephesians has unveiled the church's calling as a Colony of Heaven, an outpost radiating God's glory to earth and the heavens. In Chapter 1, we saw believers predestined in Christ to reflect His lordship, like a terrarium displaying His plan (Eph. 1:4–14, 22–23, KJV). Chapter 2 transformed us from "walking dead" to a "living display" of grace (Eph. 2:1–10). Chapter 3 revealed our cosmic purpose, uniting Jew and Gentile to showcase God's wisdom (Eph. 3:10). Chapter 4 called us to walk worthy in unity (Eph. 4:1–16) and put on the new man, renewed in mind (Eph. 4:17–32). Now, in Ephesians 5:22–6:9, Paul applies this transformation to our closest relationships—wives and husbands, children and parents, slaves and masters. These "rules for relationships" flow from the call to imitate God, walk in love, light, and wisdom, and submit mutually (Eph. 5:1–21). As citizens of heaven's colony, our relationships must reflect Christ's character, showing the world a community where His love reigns. Are we living out these roles wisely, or are we conforming to the world's patterns? Let us heed Paul's practical instructions to strengthen the body and display God's glory.

"Be ye therefore followers of God, as dear children; And walk in love, as Christ also hath loved us, and hath given himself for us an offering and a sacrifice to God for a sweetsmelling savour. But fornication, and all uncleanness, or covetousness, let it not be once named among you, as becometh saints; Neither filthiness, nor foolish talking, nor jesting, which are not convenient: but rather giving of thanks. For this ye know, that no whoremonger, nor unclean person, nor covetous man, who is an idolater, hath any inheritance in the kingdom of Christ and of God. Let no man deceive you with vain words: for because of these things cometh the wrath of God upon the children of disobedience. Be not ye therefore partakers with them. For ye were sometimes darkness, but now are ye light in the Lord: walk as children of light: (For the fruit of the Spirit is in all goodness and righteousness and truth;) Proving what is acceptable unto the Lord. And have no fellowship with the unfruitful works of darkness, but rather reprove them. For it is a shame even to speak of those things which are done of them in secret. But all things that are reproved are made manifest by the light: for whatsoever doth make manifest is light. Wherefore he saith, Awake thou that sleepest, and arise from the dead, and Christ shall give thee light. See

then that ye walk circumspectly, not as fools, but as wise, Redeeming the time, because the days are evil. Wherefore be ye not unwise, but understanding what the will of the Lord is. And be not drunk with wine, wherein is excess; but be filled with the Spirit; Speaking to yourselves in psalms and hymns and spiritual songs, singing and making melody in your heart to the Lord; Giving thanks always for all things unto God and the Father in the name of our Lord Jesus Christ; Submitting yourselves one to another in the fear of God. Wives, submit yourselves unto your own husbands, as unto the Lord. For the husband is the head of the wife, even as Christ is the head of the church: and he is the saviour of the body. Therefore as the church is subject unto Christ, so let the wives be to their own husbands in every thing. Husbands, love your wives, even as Christ also loved the church, and gave himself for it; That he might sanctify and cleanse it with the washing of water by the word, That he might present it to himself a glorious church, not having spot, or wrinkle, or any such thing; but that it should be holy and without blemish. So ought men to love their wives as their own bodies. He that loveth his wife loveth himself. For no man ever yet hated his own flesh; but nourisheth and cherisheth it, even as the Lord the church: For we are members of his body, of

his flesh, and of his bones. For this cause shall a man leave his father and mother, and shall be joined unto his wife, and they two shall be one flesh. This is a great mystery: but I speak concerning Christ and the church. Nevertheless let every one of you in particular so love his wife even as himself; and the wife see that she reverence her husband. Children, obey your parents in the Lord: for this is right. Honour thy father and mother; which is the first commandment with promise; That it may be well with thee, and thou mayest live long on the earth. And, ye fathers, provoke not your children to wrath: but bring them up in the nurture and admonition of the Lord. Servants, be obedient to them that are your masters according to the flesh, with fear and trembling, in singleness of your heart, as unto Christ; Not with eyeservice, as menpleasers; but as the servants of Christ, doing the will of God from the heart; With good will doing service, as to the Lord, and not to men: Knowing that whatsoever good thing any man doeth, the same shall he receive of the Lord, whether he be bond or free. And, ye masters, do the same things unto them, forbearing threatening: knowing that your Master also is in heaven; neither is there respect of persons with him."
Ephesians 5:1–6:9 (KJV)

Context: Walking in Love, Light, and Wisdom (Ephesians 5:1–21)

Paul begins Chapter 5 with a clarion call: "Be ye therefore followers of God, as dear children; And walk in love, as Christ also hath loved us, and hath given himself for us an offering and a sacrifice to God for a sweetsmelling savour" (Eph. 5:1–2, KJV). This is the heart of Christian living, summed up in a question that may seem cliché but carries profound weight: "What would Jesus do?" To be "followers of God" is to imitate Him as beloved children mimic a loving father, reflecting His character in every sphere of life. Christ's love—sacrificial, selfless, poured out on the cross— sets the standard. As citizens of heaven's colony, we're called to walk in this love, radiating His grace like a terrarium glowing with divine life (Ch. 2; Eph. 2:5–6, KJV). Our love isn't mere sentiment but a deliberate choice to sacrifice for others, just as Christ gave Himself as a "sweetsmelling savour" to God. In a Roman colony, settlers embodied Rome's values, transforming foreign soil (Boardman, 1980). So we, as God's outpost, embody Christ's love, transforming our homes, churches, and communities to reflect His kingdom.

Paul's warning in Ephesians 5:3, "But fornication, and all uncleanness, or covetousness, let it not be once named among you, as becometh saints" (KJV), begins with fornication—*porneia*—a Greek term encompassing all sexual immorality, including sex outside marriage and pornography. In Proverbs 7:21–27, the seductress lures a young man to "her bed" (v. 16), leading to "hell" and "death" (v. 27, KJV), a stark biblical warning of *porneia's* destructive path. Modern science echoes this: sexual activity outside God's design, including pornography, rewires the brain, releasing dopamine that fosters addiction, impairs emotional bonding, and increases anxiety and depression (Doidge, 2007; Struthers, 2009). Pornography, especially, distorts relationships, reducing others to objects and eroding the covenant love God intends for marriage (Mal. 2:14–15, KJV). Paul warns such sins have no place in heaven's colony, where we reflect Christ's holiness (Ch. 5; Eph. 4:22–24). Like a Roman colony rejecting disloyal acts to maintain Rome's honor (Levick, 1967), we flee *porneia* to display God's purity, guarding our minds and hearts to shine as His outpost in a world enslaved to lust (1 Cor. 6:18, KJV).

Paul's admonition continues by condemning *akatharsia*—uncleanness in thought and deed that defiles the heart. Proverbs 6:16–19 warns of "an heart that deviseth wicked imaginations" and "hands that shed innocent blood" (KJV), revealing uncleanness as impure motives and actions that corrupt. Modern science supports this: harboring impure thoughts, like resentment or malice, elevates stress hormones, impairing mental clarity and weakening immune function (Sapolsky, 2004). Such uncleanness festers, poisoning relationships and distorting our witness, unlike the "pure heart" God desires (Ps. 51:10, KJV). Heaven's colony must reflect Christ's holiness, putting off the old man's defilements (Ch. 5; Eph. 4:22–24). Like a Roman colony upholding Rome's purity (Levick, 1967), we reject uncleanness through repentance and prayer, guarding our thoughts to shine as God's outpost (1 John 1:9, KJV).

Paul's warning in Ephesians 5:3, "But fornication, and all uncleanness, or covetousness, let it not be once named among you, as becometh saints" (KJV), condemns *pleonexia*—covetousness, an insatiable greed that places "stuff" above God and others, violating the Tenth Commandment: "Thou shalt not covet" (Exod. 20:17, KJV). Proverbs 15:27 cautions, "He that is greedy of gain troubleth his own house" (KJV), as covetousness fractures relationships by valuing possessions over people. Modern psychology confirms this: materialism fosters isolation and anxiety, eroding relational trust (Kasser, 2002). Economically, greed drives exploitation, deepening inequality (Piketty, 2014). Consider Christ, who "thought it not robbery to be equal with God" yet left His throne to redeem us, prioritizing relationship over glory (Phil. 2:6–8, KJV). As I preached, such greed has no place in heaven's colony, where we reflect Christ's selflessness (Ch. 5; Eph. 4:22–24). Like a

Roman colony rejecting disloyalty to Rome (Levick, 1967), we renounce *pleonexia* through gratitude and generosity, prioritizing relationships to shine as God's outpost (1 Tim. 6:6–10, KJV).

Paul urges believers to "walk as children of light" (Eph. 5:8, KJV), a call to live transparently, radiating Christ's truth in a darkened world. This isn't about calling out the sins of others, but letting our transformed lives expose the contrast between light and darkness (Ch. 5; Eph. 4:22–24). The Gentiles' "darkened understanding" led to futility, living lives that would end with no eternal value (Eph. 4:17–18, KJV), but as heaven's colony, we shine like polished reflectors, vibrant with Christ's life (Ch. 2; Eph. 2:5–6). Paul recites what was probably early hymn, "Awake thou that sleepest, and arise from the dead, and Christ shall give thee light" (Eph. 5:14, KJV), echoing the resurrection power of Romans 6:4: "We are buried with him by baptism into death: that like as Christ was raised up from the dead... we also should walk in newness of life" (KJV). This call rejects lingering in the grave of our old nature, urging us to live fully alive in Christ, displaying His glory to a watching world and heavenly beings (Ch. 3; Eph. 3:10). Like a Roman colony reflecting Rome's radiance (Boardman, 1980), our lives as children of light make Christ's kingdom visible, drawing others to His truth.

Wisdom is essential to our walk: See then that ye walk circumspectly, not as fools, but as wise, Redeeming the time, because the days are evil. Wherefore be ye not unwise, but understanding what the will of the Lord is. (Eph. 5:15-17 KJV). Wisdom isn't merely having knowledge; it's the practical application of God's truth. To illustrate this, let's step back in time to the bustling streets of ancient Alexandria, home to an inventor named Hero (c. 10–70 AD). In his workshop, surrounded by the swirling dust of his trade, Hero was a man of incredible knowledge. He understood that when water was heated, it turned into steam, and that this steam held a restless, potent power. With this knowledge and understanding, he built a marvel: the *aeolipile*. It was a hollow, brass sphere that spun gracefully on its axis as twin jets of steam hissed from tiny vents. It was a fascinating creation, a prototype of the steam engine.

Yet, for all his knowledge, Hero lacked wisdom. He never saw the power of his invention as a means to do work. He left it as a curious toy, an entertaining spectacle.

Many Christians today are like Hero. They have the knowledge of a Bible trivia champion and the understanding of a systematic theologian, but, tragically, they fail to apply that knowledge to any practical use in their lives. The information is wasted without application. As W. E. Coffin once said, "The man who does not read has no advantage over the man who cannot read." Similarly, James 4:17 reminds us, "Therefore to him that knoweth to do good, and doeth it not, to him it is sin."

As heaven's colony, we are called to redeem the time, to take the knowledge of God's truth and apply it practically so that Christ's light might shine through us.

Paul's call to "redeem the time, because the days are evil" (Eph. 5:16, KJV) challenges us to assign eternal value to every moment, making each one count for Christ's kingdom. The Greek word *exagorazō*, translated "redeeming," originally described ransoming prisoners of war in Roman times, later applied to buying slaves' freedom (Thayer, 1889). When Rome redeemed a captured soldier, it wasn't because of his inherent worth but because of Rome's honor—its dignity demanded his rescue (Levick, 1967). So God redeems our time, not for our merit, but to display His glory through His colony. Picture an artist on a windswept beach, gathering driftwood others dismiss as firewood or debris. In his hands, these worthless sticks become a masterpiece, infused with beauty by his skill and vision. Likewise, God takes our fleeting moments—hours that could be lost to worldly distractions like endless scrolling or selfish pursuits—and transforms them into displays of His kingdom through Spirit-led acts of love, prayer, and service (O'Brien, 1999). The "evil" days, from the Greek *ponēros*, are not merely morally corrupt but actively harmful, like a disease spreading chaos under Satan's sway (Eph. 2:2, KJV). As citizens of heaven's colony, we counter this corruption by redeeming each moment, investing it with eternal purpose to reflect Christ's light, just as a Roman colony transformed foreign soil to mirror Rome's glory (Boardman, 1980).

Paul's charge to "be ye not unwise, but understanding what the will of the Lord is" (Eph. 5:17, KJV) calls us to seek true wisdom as citizens of heaven's colony, rooting our lives in the revealed will of God. Unlike the world's fleeting philosophies, which lead to futility (Ch. 5; Eph. 4:17–18), God's will is unveiled in His Word—the Scriptures, sharper than any two-edged sword (Heb. 4:12, KJV), and illuminated by His Spirit (John 16:13). This divine compass guides our every step, from loving our spouses to nurturing our children and serving in our workplaces (Ch. 6; Eph. 5:22–6:9). Picture a Roman colonist, studying decrees from the emperor to align every action with Rome's purpose (Levick, 1967). So we immerse ourselves in Scripture, not as a dry rulebook, but as the living voice of our King, shaping our minds to discern His will—whether to forgive a wrong, speak truth in love, or share the gospel boldly. This wisdom isn't abstract; it's practical, transforming our relationships to shine with Christ's glory (Ch. 2; O'Brien, 1999). By grounding our lives in the Word, we stand firm against the evil days' deception, displaying God's kingdom to a watching world and heavenly beings (Eph. 3:10).

Paul's command, "And be not drunk with wine, wherein is excess; but be filled with the Spirit" (Eph. 5:18, KJV), draws a sharp contrast for God's colony: drunkenness dims our witness, while spiritual fullness radiates Christ's glory. Wine's excess twists our character—kindness sours to cruelty, understanding clouds, and inhibitions crumble, leaving us open to the "evil days" (Eph. 5:16; Ch. 5). Like a Roman colonist abandoning imperial duty for a tavern's haze (Levick, 1967), drunkenness betrays our calling. Instead, Paul urges us to be "filled with the Spirit." In Greek, "Spirit" lacks the article—"the"—meaning it's not just about the Holy Spirit's presence but a life saturated with spiritual things, like Scripture, prayer, and worship (O'Brien, 1999). Think of it as filling your heart with God's treasures rather than the bottle's false comfort—no special Greek knowledge needed, just a choice to seek what lasts. Picture a Roman beacon fire, blazing high to signal the empire's strength, not doused by carelessness. As heaven's colony, we reject wine's fleeting escape, choosing instead the joy of God's Word and the peace of His will, shining brightly in our marriages, families, and workplaces to display Christ's kingdom (Ch. 6; Eph. 5:22–6:9).

Mutual submission, like soldiers in a Roman legion standing in formation, shoulder to shoulder (Levick, 1967), prepares us for the roles in Ephesians 5:22–6:9—husbands, wives, children, and workers reflecting Christ's love. This Spirit-filled life binds the colony together, our psalms and thanksgivings echoing heaven's harmony, displaying Christ's unity and glory (Ch. 4; Eph. 4:3). By living wisely, Spirit-filled, and submissive, we shine as God's outpost, transforming our world for His kingdom.

Paul's call to "speak to yourselves in psalms and hymns and spiritual songs, singing and making melody in your heart to the Lord" (Eph. 5:19, KJV) invites God's colony to harness music's power to unite and uplift, much like musicians in Roman legions inspired and guided soldiers. In Roman armies, signal musicians, called *aenatores*, played horns like the *tuba* and *cornu* to encourage troops, signal movements, and keep everyone marching in step, fostering cohesion even in battle's chaos (Roman Times, n.d.; Warren, n.d.). Likewise, as heaven's colony, we sing psalms, hymns, and spiritual songs—not just to praise God but to strengthen one another, aligning our hearts with His will. This music isn't mere performance; it's a spiritual rhythm, flowing from a Spirit-filled life (Eph. 5:18), that knits us together in joy and purpose. Picture a Roman legion, its soldiers' steps synchronized by the *cornu's* call, moving as one to reflect Rome's glory (Levick, 1967). So our worship

—whether in church, home, or workplace—encourages weary hearts, guides us in truth, and keeps our relationships in step with Christ's love, shining His kingdom's light to a watching world (O'Brien, 1999).

Paul's call to "give thanks always for all things unto God and the Father in the name of our Lord Jesus Christ" (Eph. 5:20, KJV) reveals gratitude as a cornerstone of life in God's colony, transforming our perspective in every situation—joyful or painful. Gratitude isn't just polite optimism; it's a defiant act of faith, trusting God's love and purpose even in trials, as we shine His glory to a watching world (Ch. 3; Eph. 3:10). Consider Lazarus the beggar, covered in sores, scraping by at the rich man's gate (Luke 16:19–21; Ch. 3). Did God love Lazarus? Absolutely—his suffering wasn't abandonment but a canvas for God's grace, as he rested in Abraham's bosom, a testimony to divine faithfulness (Luke 16:22). Like a Roman colony sending tribute to the emperor through storms and scarcity, proving loyalty (Levick, 1967), our constant thanks—whether in plenty or want—declares God's worth to earth and heaven. This gratitude, rooted in Christ's name, shapes our relationships, softening hearts in marriage, strengthening bonds in families, and fostering humility at work (Eph. 5:22–6:9). As heaven's colony, we give thanks not for the pain itself but for God's unchanging love, making our lives a beacon of His kingdom's hope (O'Brien, 1999).

Paul's instruction to "submit yourselves one to another in the fear of God" (Eph. 5:21, KJV) establishes mutual submission as the bedrock for all relationships in God's colony, grounding the upcoming instructions for husbands, wives, children, and workers (Eph. 5:22–6:9). This isn't about hierarchy or surrender but a humble, Christ-like choice to place others' needs above our own, reflecting the fear—awe and reverence—of God's authority (O'Brien, 1999). Picture Roman soldiers in the turtle formation, their shields interlocked to protect the unit, each soldier yielding personal space for the group's strength (Levick, 1967). So we, as heaven's colony, submit mutually— husbands sacrificing for wives, wives honoring husbands, parents nurturing children, and workers serving with integrity—not out of weakness but to mirror Christ's love (Ch. 6). This submission, flowing from a Spirit-filled life of worship and gratitude (Eph. 5:18–20), knits our relationships into a unified display of God's kingdom, shining His glory to earth and heaven (Ch. 3; Eph. 3:10). By yielding to one another, we live out the gospel, making our colony a beacon of Christ's selfless love in a self-centered world.

Wives and Husbands (Ephesians 5:22–33)

Paul begins with marriage: "Wives, submit yourselves unto your own husbands, as unto the Lord. For the husband is the head of the wife, even as Christ is the head of the church" (Eph. 5:22–23, KJV). The Greek word for "submit" (*hypotassō*) means to place oneself under, like a soldier in formation, not out of fear but reverence for Christ (Hoehner, 2002). We emphasize this is not a license for abuse. A wife's submission is to a husband who loves her sacrificially, as Paul commands: "Husbands, love your wives, even as Christ also loved the church, and gave himself for it" (Eph. 5:25, KJV). This love (*agapaō*) prioritizes her good, sanctifying and cherishing her, as Christ does the church (Eph. 5:26–29). I stress that husbands sacrifice everything—not for her whims, but for her holiness—reflecting Christ's self-giving love.

Paul roots this in Genesis: "For this cause shall a man leave his father and mother, and shall be joined unto his wife, and they two shall be one flesh" (Eph. 5:31, KJV; Gen. 2:24). Marriage mirrors Christ and the church, a "great mystery" (Eph. 5:32). As citizens of heaven's colony, husbands and wives display this divine relationship, loving and respecting each other to show the world Christ's unity with His bride. A wife's respect and a husband's love strengthen the body, making God's kingdom visible.

Children and Parents (Ephesians 6:1–4)

Paul then addresses families: "Children, obey your parents in the Lord: for this is right. Honour thy father and mother; which is the first commandment with promise" (Eph. 6:1–2, KJV; Exod. 20:12). Obedience and honor align with God's order, promising blessing: "That it may be well with thee, and thou mayest live long on the earth" (Eph. 6:3, KJV). Parents, however, must nurture thoughtfully: "And, ye fathers, provoke not your children to wrath: but bring them up in the nurture and admonition of the Lord" (Eph. 6:4, KJV). Discipline must be measured, not driven by anger, fostering godliness. In God's colony, families reflect Christ's care, with children honoring parents and parents guiding with wisdom, building a community that shines His light.

Slaves and Masters (Ephesians 6:5–9)

Finally, Paul speaks to slaves and masters, applicable today as employees and employers: "Servants, be obedient to them that are your masters according to the flesh, with fear and trembling, in singleness of your heart, as unto Christ" (Eph. 6:5, KJV). Work with integrity, not as "menpleasers" but as serving Christ (Eph. 6:6–7). A strong work ethic lifts up the Lord. When you accept a job, you are selling your time to your employer. That time no longer belongs to you, and to waste it or misuse it is theft. We should always consider our job performance as a reflection of our Master, Christ, and a witness to our coworkers, clients and employers.

Masters must "do the same things unto them, forbearing threatening: knowing that your Master also is in heaven; neither is there respect of persons with him" (Eph. 6:9, KJV). Employers treat employees with respect, recognizing Christ's impartiality. In God's colony, our work reflects His character, contributing to society with diligence and fairness, as we saw with Paul's leather-working hands (Chapter 5).

Living as Heaven's Colony

Ephesians 5:22–6:9 calls us to live in proper alignment within our relationships, like Roman soldiers in formation, each taking their place to strengthen the legion (Levick, 1967). As citizens of heaven's colony, our marriages, families, and workplaces display Christ's love and unity. A wife's submission and a husband's sacrifice mirror Christ and the church. A child's obedience and a parent's nurture reflect God's order. An employee's integrity and an employer's fairness show Christ's impartiality. These relationships, lived wisely, make heaven's culture visible, transforming our surroundings as Roman colonies did (Boardman, 1980).

Closing Challenge

Examine your relationships: Are you imitating God's love, walking as light, and redeeming time? Wives, do you honor your husbands in reverence for Christ? Husbands, do you sacrifice for your wives' good? Children, do you obey your parents? Parents, do you discipline with wisdom? Employees, do you work as unto Christ? Employers, do you treat others with fairness? As citizens of heaven's colony, let us live out these rules, reflecting Christ's kingdom in every relationship.

Prayer

Father, we thank You for calling us into Your colony, surrounded by brothers and sisters in the battle. Grant us a spirit of submission and wisdom in our roles as wives, husbands, children, parents, employees, and employers. Help us live wisely, reflecting Christ's love and unity, that Your kingdom may shine through us. In Jesus' name,

Amen.

References

Boardman, J. (1980). *The Greeks Overseas*. Thames & Hudson.

Bruce, F. F. (1984). *The Epistles to the Colossians, to Philemon, and to the Ephesians*. Eerdmans.

Doidge, N. (2007). *The Brain That Changes Itself: Stories of Personal Triumph from the Frontiers of Brain Science*. Penguin Books.

Kasser, T. (2002). *The High Price of Materialism*. MIT Press.

Levick, B. (1967). *Roman Colonies in Southern Asia Minor*. Oxford University Press.

O'Brien, P. T. (1999). *The Letter to the Ephesians*. Eerdmans.

Piketty, T. (2014). *Capital in the 21st Century*. Harvard University Press.

Roman Times. (n.d.). *Signal Musicians in the Roman Legions*. Retrieved from http://ancientimes.blogspot.com

Sapolsky, R. M. (2004). *Why Zebras Don't Get Ulcers: The Acclaimed Guide to Stress, Stress-Related Diseases, and Coping*. Henry Holt and Company.

Struthers, W. M. (2009). *Wired for Intimacy: How Pornography Hijacks the Male Brain*

Warren, B. D. (n.d.). *Communications in the Roman Legions*. Retrieved from http:// bacildonovanwarren.com

7

Standing Firm as Heaven's Colony

Our journey through Ephesians has unveiled the church's glorious calling as a Colony of Heaven—an outpost radiating God's kingdom in a world estranged from Him. In Chapter 1, we marveled at our predestination in Christ to reflect His lordship, like a terrarium showcasing His eternal plan (Eph. 1:4–14, 22–23, KJV). Chapter 2 transformed us from "walking dead" to a "living display" of His grace, surrendered to His authority (Eph. 2:1–10). Chapter 3 revealed our cosmic purpose, uniting Jew and Gentile to display God's wisdom to heavenly beings (Eph. 3:10). Chapter 4 called us to walk worthy in unity, growing into Christ's likeness (Eph. 4:1–16), while Chapter 5 urged us to put off the old man and live transformed lives (Eph. 4:17–32). Chapter 6 applied this transformation to our relationships, reflecting Christ's love in marriage, family, and work (Eph. 5:22–6:9). Now, in Ephesians 6:10–24, Paul equips us to stand firm as God's colony, clothed in His armor to withstand the enemy's schemes. As citizens of heaven's colony, we are not defenseless settlers but armed soldiers, empowered by Christ's strength to defend His outpost and proclaim His gospel boldly.

This chapter challenges us: Are we standing firm, equipped with God's armor, or are we vulnerable to the world's attacks? Let us heed Paul's call to don the full armor of God, standing as a unified colony to display His victory to earth and the heavens.

"Finally, my brethren, be strong in the Lord, and in the power of his might. Put on the whole armour of God, that ye may be able to stand against the wiles of the devil. For we wrestle not against flesh and blood, but against principalities, against powers, against the rulers of the darkness of this world, against spiritual wickedness in high places. Wherefore take unto you the whole armour of God, that ye may be able to withstand in the evil day, and having done all, to stand. Stand therefore, having your loins girt about with truth, and having on the breastplate of righteousness; And your feet shod with the preparation of the gospel of peace; Above all, taking the shield of faith, wherewith ye shall be able to quench all the fiery darts of the wicked. And take the helmet of salvation, and the sword of the Spirit, which is the word of God: Praying always with all prayer and supplication in the Spirit, and watching thereunto with all perseverance and supplication for all saints; And for me, that utterance may be given unto me, that I may open my mouth boldly, to make known the

mystery of the gospel, For which I am an ambassador in bonds: that therein I may speak boldly, as I ought to speak. But that ye also may know my affairs, and how I do, Tychicus, a beloved brother and faithful minister in the Lord, shall make known to you all things: Whom I have sent unto you for the same purpose, that ye might know our affairs, and that he might comfort your hearts. Peace be to the brethren, and love with faith, from God the Father and the Lord Jesus Christ. Grace be with all them that love our Lord Jesus Christ in sincerity. Amen" (Eph. 6:10–24, KJV).

The Battle for the Colony

Paul begins, "Finally, my brethren, be strong in the Lord, and in the power of his might" (Eph. 6:10, KJV). Paul uses "finally" to mean "and as for the rest," signaling a culmination of his teaching. He's addressed our life in the body (Ch. 4), our relationships (Ch. 6), and now he equips us for "everything else"—living as God's colony in a hostile world. As a prisoner in Rome, chained to a Roman soldier under house arrest (Acts 28:30–31, KJV), Paul had ample time to observe the soldier's armor. Day after day, a new guard would be shackled to him, unable to escape his witness. I can imagine Paul studying the soldier's gear—belt, breastplate, shield— while the Holy Spirit stirred his heart to see a spiritual parallel. The Lord gave Paul a gift for taking everyday things, like a soldier's armor, and using them to unveil divine truth. Here, he casts the church as an armed outpost, not strolling carelessly through life but standing firm as soldiers of Christ, equipped to defend heaven's colony.

We often walk through life as if nothing can harm us, expecting the world to shower us with accolades. But we shouldn't be surprised when opposition comes. Jesus warned, "If the world hate you, ye know that it hated me before it hated you" (John 15:18, KJV). The world's hostility isn't a surprise; it's a promise. Yet, we're not defenseless. God has equipped us with His armor to stand against the "wiles of the devil" (Eph. 6:11, KJV). As citizens of heaven's colony, we're not settlers hoping for peace but soldiers prepared for battle, called to display Christ's victory in a world under the sway of "the prince of the power of the air" (Eph. 2:2, KJV).

Paul clarifies our true enemy: "For we wrestle not against flesh and blood, but against principalities, against powers, against the rulers of the darkness of this world, against spiritual wickedness in high places" (Eph. 6:12, KJV). I won't speculate on the hierarchy of these spiritual forces—whether principalities or powers differ in rank. What matters is that they are real, actively working against us, manipulating unbelievers in our families, workplaces, or schools to oppose us. Our neighbors, coworkers, or even those who persecute us aren't the enemy. Their rejection of truth puts them in a far worse state than any harm they can do to us. Our hearts should break for them, not harden against them. We don't hate our persecutors; we pray for them, knowing their destiny without Christ is far graver than any trial we face (Luke 23:34, KJV). Our battle is spiritual, and God's armor equips us to stand as His colony, radiating His truth and love in a dark world.

The Full Armor of God (Ephesians 6:13–17)

Paul urges, "Wherefore take unto you the whole armour of God, that ye may be able to withstand in the evil day, and having done all, to stand" (Eph. 6:13, KJV). We don't put on the armor halfway. The "evil day" may be a specific time of persecution or simply any moment Satan attacks—temptation, discouragement, or opposition. We don't wait for the fiery darts to whistle past our ears to scramble for our gear. Like Roman soldiers who donned their armor daily, we wear God's armor every day, ready for battle whenever it comes. In a Roman colony, soldiers were always prepared, their presence a visible reminder of Rome's authority (Levick, 1967). Likewise, as heaven's colony, we stand equipped, displaying Christ's lordship in a world that rejects Him.

Paul details the armor, each piece reflecting Christ's provision for His body:

Belt of Truth: "Stand therefore, having your loins girt about with truth" (Eph. 6:14, KJV). The Roman soldier's belt was heavy and thick, the foundation for all other gear. The sword hung from it, the breastplate attached to it—without the belt, everything fell apart. Paul calls this the "belt of truth." For the Christian, truthfulness is foundational. It's not just avoiding lies but living what we believe, as we saw in Chapter 5 (Eph. 4:25, KJV). In a Roman colony, fidelity to Rome's standards held the community together (Boardman, 1980). Similarly, our commitment to Christ's truth—His Word and character—anchors our lives, ensuring our actions reflect our King. A life of honesty strengthens the colony's witness, making heaven's culture visible.

Breastplate of Righteousness: "And having on the breastplate of righteousness" (Eph. 6:14, KJV). The breastplate covered the heart, protecting the will. What did Paul mean by "heart"? In our modern world, we think of the heart as the seat of emotions—love, passion, or sentiment. We say, "I love you with all my heart," picturing warm feelings. But in the New Testament, the Greek understanding of the heart (*kardia*) is quite different. The heart was the seat of the will—the center of decision-making, resolve, and purpose. As O'Brien notes, "In biblical thought, the heart is the source of a person's choices and actions, the core of their being where intentions are formed" (O'Brien, 1999, p. 477). It's where we decide to obey God or follow our own desires. The bowels (*splagchna*), not the heart, were associated with emotions—deep feelings like compassion or mercy, as when Paul speaks of his "bowels of mercies" (Phil. 1:8, KJV) or Jesus was "moved with compassion" (Matt. 9:36, KJV). The mind (*nous*), was the seat of thought and imagination, as we explore in Appendix B with the "renewed mind" (Eph. 4:23, KJV).This distinction matters because the breastplate of righteousness protects our will—our capacity to choose what's right. In Christ, we're clothed with His righteousness (Eph. 4:24, KJV), enabling us to make godly decisions, not just expedient ones. Righteousness means doing what's right every time, not what's convenient. When the heart, as the seat of the will, is guarded by righteousness, our choices align with Christ's character, not the world's deceitful lusts (Ch. 5). Contrast this with today's view: if we see the heart as mere emotion, we might think righteousness is about feeling good or being sincere. "Follow your heart" is common but foolish advice. But sincerity without godly choices can lead us astray. A Roman soldier's breastplate was solid, immovable, guarding his life. So righteousness guards our will, making decisions easier because they're already made: "I will do what's right." As heaven's colony, our righteous choices shine like a soldier's polished breastplate, testifying to Christ's transforming power before a watching world (Hoehner, 2002).

Feet Shod with the Gospel of Peace: "And your feet shod with the preparation of the gospel of peace" (Eph. 6:15, KJV). The Greek word *hetoimasiade* notes readiness, a deliberate equipping for battle, like a soldier fitting sandals with hobnails (*clavi*) for grip (*Thayer's Greek Lexicon*, 1889). Picture a Roman legion on a windswept Judean hillside, the ground treacherous with rain-soaked clay and jagged stones. Their *caligae*, studded with iron nails, bite into the earth, anchoring them against the enemy's charge or the slip of rugged slopes. Mud clings to their sandals, yet they stand unshaken, their footing sure, ready to hold the line or advance. Each soldier has painstakingly driven those nails into his soles, not once but repeatedly, ensuring they'll grip when battle comes. So the gospel of peace equips us with *hetoimasia*—a steadfast readiness rooted in Christ's victory (John 16:33, KJV). This gospel gives us traction, not to slip in the world's chaos but to stand firm, proclaiming the peace Christ won on the cross (Eph. 2:14, KJV).

This readiness isn't a passing knowledge of the gospel, like a glance at a soldier's gear before battle. It's a daily, deliberate act—like a soldier driving nails into his sandals, checking each one for strength. We must drive the nails of the gospel into our lives through repeated study of God's Word, fervent prayer, and living out Christ's peace. Meditate on the cross, where He reconciled us to God (Eph. 2:16, KJV). Let His promises sink deep, fortifying your heart against doubt or fear. As you face trials—temptation, rejection, or despair—these gospel nails give you grip to stand firm and advance, sharing Christ's peace with a world in conflict. In a Roman colony, soldiers' sure footing declared Rome's unyielding presence (Levick, 1967). As heaven's colony, our gospel-grounded stance displays Christ's triumph, enabling us to face opposition with confidence and proclaim His kingdom with boldness (O'Brien, 1999).

Shield of Faith: "Above all, taking the shield of faith, wherewith ye shall be able to quench all the fiery darts of the wicked" (Eph. 6:16, KJV). The Roman shield was large, curved, and designed to interlock in the "tortoise" formation, protecting the entire unit. Our faith isn't just personal—it strengthens those around us. When we trust Christ's promises, we shield our brothers and sisters, quenching Satan's darts of doubt, fear, or temptation. In a Roman colony, soldiers' unity was their strength (Levick, 1967). So it is with us: our collective faith fortifies the colony, displaying Christ's power to a watching world and heavenly beings (Eph. 3:10, KJV).

Helmet of Salvation: the helmet protects the mind— our thoughts and imagination, the seat of the nous in

Greek thinking, where we envision and ponder (Appendix B; Eph. 4:23, KJV). In a Roman legion, a soldier's helmet was more than a cover for his head; it was a masterpiece of design, forged to withstand crushing blows from swords or stones, its reinforced crest and cheek guards absorbing the shock of battle (Bruce, 1984). Yet the helmet did more—it shaped the soldier's vision. Its curved sides and narrow visor deliberately limited peripheral sight, blocking distractions from the chaos of clashing armies or taunting foes. This forced the soldier's eyes forward, fixed on the commander's standard or the enemy before him, ensuring focus amid the fray. Picture a centurion on a Galilean battlefield, dust swirling, spears flashing. His helmet narrows his gaze to the task—hold the line, advance with the legion—undeterred by the clamor at his flanks.

> **See Appendix B:The Renewed Mind: Sober Thinking and the Helmet of Salvation**
>
> **For a fuller discussion.**

So the helmet of salvation guards our mind against the world's lies, as we saw with the Gentiles' "vanity of their mind" (Eph. 4:17, KJV; Ch. 5). It aligns our thoughts with Christ's, renewing our imagination to envision His kingdom, not the world's fleeting lures. Like the Roman helmet, salvation focuses our spiritual vision, blocking the peripheral distractions of doubt, fear, or temptation that vie for our attention. We fix our eyes on Christ, "the author and finisher of our faith" (Heb. 12:2, KJV), undeterred by the enemy's taunts.

In a Roman colony, a soldier's helmet declared his allegiance to Rome, gleaming as a symbol of authority (Levick, 1967). Our salvation proclaims we belong to Christ, enabling us to think His thoughts and live as His outpost, displaying His glory to a watching world and heavenly beings (Eph. 3:10, KJV). Each morning, as we don this helmet, we commit to focus on His truth, letting His Word and Spirit shape our minds to reflect heaven's colony.

Sword of the Spirit: "And the sword of the Spirit, which is the word of God" (Eph. 6:17, KJV). This is our offensive weapon. When Jesus faced Satan's temptations, He wielded Scripture, quoting Deuteronomy to defeat the enemy (Matt. 4:4–10, KJV). If Christ relied on God's Word, how much more must we? We have no other weapon but the Word. "Faith cometh by hearing, and hearing by the word of God" (Rom. 10:17, KJV). We can't reason or entertain someone into faith—only the Spirit, through the Word, pierces hearts. As heaven's colony, we wield this sword to advance Christ's kingdom, cutting through lies to reveal His truth.

This Word is no ordinary blade. By it, God framed the worlds, bringing order from chaos: "By the word of the Lord were the heavens made; and all the host of them by the breath of his mouth" (Ps. 33:6, KJV; Heb. 11:3). Its creative power established the universe, and now it establishes Christ's kingdom through us, His colony, transforming hearts and ordering lives under His rule. The Word is "quick, and powerful, and sharper than any twoedged sword, piercing even to the dividing asunder of soul and spirit, and of the joints and marrow, and is a discerner of the thoughts and intents of the heart" (Heb. 4:12, KJV). Like a Roman soldier's *gladius*, honed to cleave through armor, the Word penetrates the deepest recesses of the human soul, exposing lies, convicting sin, and aligning us with Christ's truth. Picture a legionary in a Galilean valley, his sword flashing in the sun, striking with precision to fell the enemy. So we, as heaven's soldiers, wield the Word to cut through the world's deceptions—doubt, pride, or fear—revealing the gospel's light.

When Christ returns, "out of his mouth goeth a sharp sword, that with it he should smite the nations" (Rev. 19:15, KJV). This sword, His Word, is His conquering weapon, securing His final victory. As His colony, we wield that same Word now, empowered by the Spirit to advance His kingdom. Each time we proclaim Scripture, pray its promises, or live its truth, we strike blows against the enemy's lies, displaying Christ's lordship to a watching world and heavenly beings (Eph. 3:10, KJV). We don't persuade by human wit but rely on the Spirit's power through the Word.

In a Roman colony, a soldier's sword marked his authority to enforce Rome's will (Levick, 1967). So the sword of the Spirit marks us as Christ's ambassadors, equipped to establish His reign. Let us grip this blade daily—through study, prayer, and bold witness— knowing it never fails.

Prayer as the Colony's Lifeline (Ephesians 6:18–20)

Paul continues, "Praying always with all prayer and supplication in the Spirit, and watching thereunto with all perseverance and supplication for all saints; And for me, that utterance may be given unto me, that I may open my mouth boldly, to make known the mystery of the gospel, For which I am an ambassador in bonds: that therein I may speak boldly, as I ought to speak" (Eph. 6:18–19, KJV). As I preached, prayer keeps us in contact with headquarters—our King, Jesus Christ. It's not just asking for strength but learning where we're weak and seeking God's power. Yet Paul's words, layered with modifiers, reveal the depth of this lifeline, equipping heaven's colony to stand firm in spiritual battle.

"Praying always" calls us to unceasing communion with God, like a Roman outpost maintaining a constant signal to the emperor's throne (Levick, 1967). Prayer isn't confined to morning devotions or

Sunday services but pulses through every moment, as Paul urged, "Pray without ceasing" (1 Thess. 5:17, KJV). Whether in joy or trial, we stay connected to Christ, our Commander. "All prayer and supplication" expands this, encompassing every form of prayer— praising God's glory, confessing our sins, giving thanks for His grace, and pleading for needs. Imagine a soldier's dispatches, varied yet urgent, covering worship and requests alike. As heaven's colony, our prayers weave adoration, confession, and supplication into a tapestry that glorifies Christ and sustains His body.

"In the Spirit" ensures our prayers are not mere words but Spirit-led cries, guided by His power. "Likewise the Spirit also helpeth our infirmities: for we know not what we should pray for as we ought" (Rom. 8:26, KJV). The Spirit aligns our prayers with God's will, making them effective in battle, like a soldier following precise orders from headquarters. "Watching thereunto" demands vigilance, as a sentinel on a Roman watchtower, eyes scanning the horizon for threats or signals. We stay alert to the enemy's schemes and the needs of God's people, praying with focus, not rote routine. "All perseverance" calls us to endure, like a legionary holding a post through a long siege, trusting God's timing even when answers tarry. Jesus taught, "Men ought always to pray, and not to faint" (Luke 18:1, KJV), urging steadfastness. "All saints" binds us to every believer, from our local church to the global body, reflecting the unity of "one body, and one Spirit" (Eph. 4:4, KJV). Our prayers interlock like Roman shields, strengthening the colony as one.

Even Paul, the apostle, sought prayer as an "ambassador in bonds," asking for boldness to proclaim the "mystery of the gospel" (Eph. 6:19–20, KJV). Chained to Roman soldiers, his witness never wavered; his chains amplified it, reaching even Caesar's household (Acts 28:30–31; Phil. 4:22, KJV). Picture Paul, shackled yet speaking, his words piercing hearts as the Spirit wielded them. So we, as heaven's colony, pray for our fellow soldiers—pastors, missionaries, neighbors, fellow church members— lifting their needs with perseverance. Our prayers sustain the body's mission, binding us together and empowering us to speak boldly, displaying Christ's glory to earth and heavenly beings (Eph. 3:10, KJV). Like a Roman colony's unbroken line to Rome, our Spirit-led, vigilant prayers ensure we stand as Christ's outpost, unshaken by the enemy's assaults.

God hasn't sent us into battle unarmed. From our feet to our head, He's equipped us with armor that cannot fail and a sword—the Word—that no enemy can withstand. Our prayers, guided by the Spirit, are a secure line to heaven, unintercepted by the enemy. Like a Roman colony fortified against barbarian attacks, the church stands as God's outpost, displaying His victory through our unity, faith, and bold witness (Graham, 1983).

The Colony's Faithful Witness (Ephesians 6:21–24)

Paul closes, "But that ye also may know my affairs, and how I do, Tychicus, a beloved brother and faithful minister in the Lord, shall make known to you all things" (Eph. 6:21, KJV). Tychicus, who carried this letter (Eph. 6:21–22; Col. 4:7–9, KJV), embodies the colony's unity, connecting believers across cities with news of Paul's ministry. Paul's final words—"Peace be to the brethren, and love with faith, from God the Father and the Lord Jesus Christ. Grace be with all them that love our Lord Jesus Christ in sincerity" (Eph. 6:23–24, KJV)—seal the epistle with a blessing. This reflects the colony's mission: to live in peace, love, and faith, radiating Christ's grace to a world in need.

Imagine a Roman colony under siege, its soldiers standing shoulder to shoulder, shields interlocked, swords gleaming. Their unity and readiness declared Rome's power. So we, as heaven's colony, stand firm, our faith interlocked, our prayers fervent, our witness bold. The terrarium of Chapter 2 shines still—a miniature universe under Christ's rule, unshaken by the enemy's darts because we're clothed in His armor (Eph. 1:22–23, KJV). Our lives, like Paul's, are not about personal ease but about displaying God's glory, as Lazarus did (Ch. 3; Luke 16:19–31, KJV), to earth and the heavens.

Living as Heaven's Colony

Ephesians 6:10–24 is a rallying cry to stand firm as God's colony. We're not aimless settlers but soldiers equipped with Christ's strength, truth, and Word. The armor isn't decorative—it's functional, protecting us to proclaim the gospel boldly. We don't wait for the battle to don our gear; we wear it daily, ready for the evil day. Our enemy isn't flesh and blood but spiritual forces, and our response isn't hatred but prayer for those lost in darkness. Like Paul, chained yet preaching, we're ambassadors in a hostile world, making Christ's kingdom visible through our unity and witness.

Consider again the terrarium—a fragile yet vibrant display of life, sustained by Christ's power. Or picture Paul, chained to a soldier, studying his armor while sharing the gospel. His chains didn't weaken his mission; they strengthened it, just as our trials can amplify our witness when we stand in God's armor. Every piece—truth, righteousness, peace, faith, salvation, the Word—equips us to reflect Christ's lordship, as Roman colonists reflected Rome's glory (Levick, 1967). Our prayers bind us to Him and each other, ensuring the colony stands firm.

Closing Challenge

Are you standing firm as a citizen of heaven's colony, clothed in God's armor? Or are you vulnerable, caught off guard by the enemy's schemes? Examine your life: Is truth your foundation, righteousness your guide, the gospel your traction? Is your faith shielding others, your mind guarded by salvation, your hand wielding the Word? Are you praying for your fellow soldiers, seeking boldness like Paul? As God's colony, let us commit to donning the full armor daily, standing together to display Christ's victory to a watching world and heavenly beings.

Prayer

Father, we are so thankful that You have not sent us into battle unarmed. You've equipped us with Your whole armor—truth, righteousness, peace, faith, salvation, and Your Word. Grant us grace to put it on every day, standing firm as Your colony. Fill us with Your Spirit to pray for one another and speak Your gospel boldly. May our lives, like Paul's, proclaim Your glory, even in chains. Unto You be glory in the church by Christ Jesus, world without end. In Jesus' name we pray,

Amen.

References

Boardman, J. (1980). *The Greeks Overseas*. Thames & Hudson.

Bruce, F. F. (1984). *The Epistles to the Colossians, to Philemon, and to the Ephesians*. Eerdmans.

Graham, A. J. (1983). *Colony and Mother City in Ancient Greece*. Manchester University Press.

Hoehner, H. W. (2002). *Ephesians: An Exegetical Commentary*. Baker Academic.

Levick, B. (1967). *Roman Colonies in Southern Asia Minor*. Oxford University Press.

O'Brien, P. T. (1999). *The Letter to the Ephesians*. Eerdmans.

Thayer, J. H. (1889). *Greek-English Lexicon of the New Testament*. Harper & Brothers.

8

Conclusion: Shining as Heaven's Colony

Throughout our journey in Colony of Heaven, we've explored Paul's letter to the Ephesians as a divine blueprint for the church—an outpost of God's kingdom radiating His glory in a world estranged from Him. From the opening verses, we marveled at our predestination in Christ, chosen to reflect His lordship like a terrarium showcasing His eternal plan (Ch. 1; Eph. 1:4–14, KJV). We were transformed from "walking dead" to a "living display" of His grace, surrendered to His authority (Ch. 2; Eph. 2:1–10). In Chapter 3, we discovered our cosmic purpose, uniting Jew and Gentile to display God's wisdom to heavenly beings (Eph. 3:10). Chapter 4 called us to walk worthy in unity, growing into Christ's likeness (Eph. 4:1–16), while Chapter 5 urged us to put off the old man and live transformed lives (Eph. 4:17–32). Chapter 6 applied this transformation to relationships, reflecting Christ's love in marriage, family, and work (Eph. 5:22–6:9). In Chapter 7, we donned the full armor of God, standing firm as armed soldiers against spiritual opposition (Eph. 6:10–24).

Now, as we conclude, we stand at the culmination of Paul's vision: a church that shines as a Colony of Heaven, displaying Christ's glory to earth and the heavens through transformed lives, unified love, and bold witness. This chapter challenges us: Are we living as citizens of this colony, radiating His kingdom, or are we dimmed by the world's shadows? Let us recommit to shine as God's outpost, equipped by His Word and Spirit to fulfill our calling.

> *"Now unto him that is able to do exceeding abundantly above all that we ask or think, according to the power that worketh in us, Unto him be glory in the church by Christ Jesus throughout all ages, world without end. Amen"* *(Eph. 3:20–21, KJV).*

The Colony's Calling: Glory in the Church

Paul's doxology in Ephesians 3:20–21 captures the heart of our calling as a Colony of Heaven: to give God glory "in the church by Christ Jesus" forever. As I've said throughout this series, the church is not a building or a Sunday gathering but a living community, an outpost of heaven's kingdom planted in a hostile world. In a Roman colony, settlers transformed foreign soil into a mirror of Rome's culture, their lives testifying to the emperor's reign (Levick, 1967). So we, as God's colony, transform our world by reflecting Christ's lordship. This isn't about personal piety alone but a collective mission—Jew and Gentile, rich and poor, united as one body (Ch. 3; Eph. 2:14–16, KJV). Our lives, like the terrarium of Chapter 2, are a miniature universe under Christ's rule, displaying His grace to a watching world and heavenly beings (Eph. 3:10).

This glory begins with God's eternal plan. In Chapter 1, we saw how He chose us "before the foundation of the world" to be holy and blameless, predestined to adoption through Christ (Eph. 1:4–5, KJV; Appendix A). This isn't a cold doctrine but a warm assurance: we belong to Him, crafted for His purpose. Like driftwood shaped by the Artist, our lives are molded by His grace to reflect His beauty (Ch. 1). Yet this calling demands transformation. Chapter 2 showed us as "dead in trespasses and sins," enslaved to the world's prince (Eph. 2:1–2, KJV). But God, rich in mercy, made us alive, raising us to sit with Christ in heavenly places (Eph. 2:5–6). This transformation isn't cosmetic—it's a new creation, putting off the old man's deceitful lusts and putting on the new man, created in righteousness (Ch. 5; Eph. 4:22–24).

Our unity as a colony magnifies this glory. In Chapter 4, Paul urged us to walk worthy, keeping "the unity of the Spirit in the bond of peace" (Eph. 4:3, KJV). Like Roman soldiers' interlocked shields in the tortoise formation (Ch. 7), our love and humility bind us together, making Christ's kingdom visible. This unity isn't sameness but diversity—different gifts, roles, and backgrounds, yet one body under one Head (Eph. 4:11–16). Chapter 6 extended this to relationships, where husbands love sacrificially, wives submit in honor, children obey, and workers serve as unto Christ (Eph. 5:22–6:9). These acts of love aren't mere duties but displays of heaven's culture, shining in homes and workplaces.

The cosmic scope of our calling, unveiled in Chapter 3, elevates this mission. The church declares God's manifold wisdom "to the principalities and powers in heavenly places" (Eph. 3:10, KJV). As I shared, this is no small thing—angels and demons watch as we, frail humans, embody Christ's victory. Our unity, love, and transformed lives preach a sermon to the heavens, testifying that Christ's cross has triumphed (Col. 2:15, KJV). Like Lazarus raised from death to display God's glory (Ch. 3; John 11:40, KJV), we live to showcase His power.

Equipped to Stand Firm

This calling isn't without opposition. Chapter 7 equipped us with the full armor of God to stand against the "wiles of the devil" (Eph. 6:11, KJV). As I stated, our enemy isn't flesh and blood but spiritual forces manipulating a world in darkness (Eph. 6:12). Yet we're not defenseless. The belt of truth anchors us, the breastplate of righteousness guards our will, the gospel of peace gives us traction, the shield of faith protects our community, the helmet of salvation renews our mind, and the sword of the Spirit—God's Word—pierces lies (Eph. 6:14–17). Prayer, our lifeline to headquarters, binds us to Christ and each other, empowering bold witness (Eph. 6:18–20). Like Paul, chained yet preaching to Roman soldiers (Acts 28:30–31, KJV), we shine in trials, our lives amplifying Christ's gospel.

The renewed mind, explored in Appendix B, is central to this stand. The Gentiles' "vanity of their mind" led to futility (Eph. 4:17–18, KJV), but the Spirit and Word transform us to think soberly, seeing life through God's lens (Rom. 12:2–3; Appendix B). This isn't passive—it's a daily discipline, like a soldier donning his helmet each morning. The Word, "quick, and powerful, and sharper than any twoedged sword" (Heb. 4:12, KJV), recalibrates our compass, while the Spirit guides us into truth (John 16:13). As I shared, it's not "garbage in, garbage out" but truth in, truth out. This renewed mind enables us to live distinctly, reflecting heaven's values in a world of chaos.

Shining in a Dark World

How do we shine as heaven's colony? By living out Paul's vision in every sphere. In our churches, we pursue unity, using our gifts to build up the body (Ch. 4; Eph. 4:12). In our homes, we model Christ's love, whether as spouses, parents, or children (Ch. 6). In our workplaces, we serve as unto the Lord, not men

(Eph. 6:7). In the world, we stand firm, wielding the Word to cut through lies and praying for those lost in darkness (Ch. 7). As I've shared, our hearts should break for our persecutors, not harden against them, for their destiny without Christ is far graver than our trials (Luke 23:34, KJV). Our witness—through words, actions, and love—makes Christ's kingdom visible, like a Roman colony transforming its region with Rome's culture (Boardman, 1980).

Consider again the terrarium from Chapter 2—a fragile glass sphere, yet vibrant with life under Christ's rule. Though storms rage outside, its light shines unshaken, sustained by His power. Or picture a Roman colony, its soldiers standing shoulder to shoulder, shields interlocked, helmets gleaming, proclaiming Rome's glory. So we, as heaven's colony, stand united, armed with God's truth, our minds renewed, our lives radiating His glory. I recall a story from my church: a lady asked me to visit her father, for whose spiritual condition she was concerned. She warned me the last preacher to visit was thrown off his porch, breaking his arm. I went anyway, and we had a pleasant conversation about fishing and hunting, but he wouldn't hear the gospel. For years, I stopped by, talking, praying, yet he remained closed. Then I heard he was hospitalized in another city. I prayed, fearing he might die without Christ. That Sunday, his daughter stopped me at church, joyfully sharing that her father had told her to let me know he had trusted Christ. That's the colony's mission—not to curse the darkness but to shine Christ's light through persistent prayer and witness, trusting the Spirit to work.

This shining isn't about perfection but dependence. Paul's doxology reminds us that God works "exceeding abundantly above all that we ask or think" (Eph. 3:20, KJV). Our weakness is His canvas—He uses frail vessels to display His power (2 Cor. 4:7). As Again, we don't wait for the evil day to don our armor; we wear it daily, ready to stand, pray, and proclaim. The Word that framed the worlds (Heb. 11:3) and will conquer at Christ's return (Rev. 19:15) empowers us now to live as His outpost.

Living as Heaven's Colony

Ephesians calls us to a high calling: to be a Colony of Heaven, displaying God's glory through transformed lives, unified love, and bold witness. This isn't a solitary task but a communal one, as we interlock shields, pray for all saints, and wield the Word together. Our transformed minds see eternity where the world sees futility; our love unites where the world divides; our witness proclaims Christ where the world denies Him. Like Paul, chained yet preaching, we shine in trials, our lives a sermon to earth and heaven. The terrarium endures storms, the soldier stands firm, the colony radiates its King's glory. This is our mission—to live so distinctly that the world sees Christ, and the heavens marvel at His wisdom.

Closing Challenge

Examine your life: Are you shining as a citizen of heaven's colony, or are you dimmed by the world's shadows? Is your mind renewed by the Word and Spirit, your relationships marked by Christ's love, your witness bold with His truth? Commit today to live as God's outpost—read Scripture daily to anchor your thoughts, pray for your brothers and sisters, and share the gospel boldly, even in chains. Let us give God glory in the church, trusting His power to work through us "world without end" (Eph. 3:21, KJV).

Prayer

Father, we thank You for calling us as Your Colony of Heaven, chosen to display Your glory. Renew our minds by Your Word and Spirit, unite us in love, and equip us with Your armor to stand firm. Grant us boldness to proclaim Your gospel, even in trials, that Christ's kingdom may shine through us to earth and the heavens. Unto You be glory in the church by Christ Jesus forever. In Jesus' name,

Amen.

References

Boardman, J. (1980). *The Greeks Overseas*. Thames & Hudson.

Bruce, F. F. (1984). *The Epistles to the Colossians, to Philemon, and to the Ephesians*. Eerdmans.

Graham, A. J. (1983). *Colony and Mother City in Ancient Greece*. Manchester University Press.

Hoehner, H. W. (2002). *Ephesians: An Exegetical Commentary*. Baker Academic.

Levick, B. (1967). *Roman Colonies in Southern Asia Minor*. Oxford University Press.

O'Brien, P. T. (1999). *The Letter to the Ephesians*. Eerdmans.

Thayer, J. H. (1889). *Greek-English Lexicon of the New Testament*. Harper & Brothers.

Appendix A

Predestination: Privilege or Purpose?

Few doctrines in Scripture have generated as much discussion—and division—as predestination. For centuries, theologians have debated whether Paul's words in Ephesians 1:4–5 teach an unconditional, individual election to salvation, or something else entirely. But if we read Ephesians on its own terms, through the lens of its first-century audience and its sweeping theme of the church as a Colony of Heaven, a different picture emerges—one of calling and commission rather than elitism and exclusion.

Paul writes, "According as he hath chosen us in him before the foundation of the world, that we should be holy and without blame before him in love: Having predestinated us unto the adoption of children by Jesus Christ to himself, according to the good pleasure of his will" (Eph. 1:4–5, KJV). Notice the prepositions: "in him" and "unto adoption". Paul is not primarily discussing individuals being selected while others are passed over. He is describing the destiny of those who are in Christ—that all who belong to Him are chosen for holiness, adoption, and mission.

Throughout Ephesians, election is corporate and vocational. God has always chosen a people to represent Him: Israel in the Old Testament, the church in the New. In Christ, that calling expands to Jew and Gentile alike (Eph. 3:6). The point of being "chosen" is not to boast in privilege but to embrace responsibility —living as citizens of heaven's colony in a world estranged from God. In other words, predestination is about God's plan and purpose, not our personal status.

This perspective shifts our posture. Rather than speculating about who is "in" or "out," we rejoice that God's plan from eternity was to create a people redeemed by Christ, adopted into His family, and empowered by His Spirit to display His glory. It's less like a lottery ticket to heaven and more like being drafted onto a team with a mission—to bring the culture of heaven to earth.

Chosen "In Him": The Corporate Dimension

When Paul says "he hath chosen us in him before the foundation of the world" (Eph. 1:4, KJV), the focus is not on isolated individuals but on the community of believers "in Christ." In the New Testament, to be "in Christ" means to be joined to Him by faith, incorporated into His body. Those who are in Christ share His blessings, His calling, and His destiny.

In the Old Testament, God chose Israel not because they were better than other nations but because of His covenant love (Deut. 7:7–8). He called them to be a "kingdom of priests" (Exod. 19:6)—a mediating nation bringing His light to the Gentiles (Isa. 42:6). In the same way, the church is now chosen in Christ to show forth His praises (1 Pet. 2:9). Election is about representing God to the world, not excluding the world from God.

Predestined "Unto Adoption": The Vocational Dimension

Paul continues, "Having predestinated us unto the adoption of children by Jesus Christ to himself" (Eph. 1:5, KJV). Predestination here is not about who gets saved but about the goal God set for all who believe: adoption into His family and conformity to Christ's image. Romans 8:29–30 makes the same point: "For whom he did foreknow, he also did predestinate to be conformed to the image of his Son." The predestination is to a purpose—holiness, adoption, conformity—not to exclusion or fatalism.

In the Roman world, adoption was a public, legal act granting the full rights of an heir to someone not born into the family. Once adopted, you received a new name, new status, and a guaranteed inheritance. Paul draws on this image to show that every believer in Christ has been predestined to full family rights—not merely as future hope but present reality. This is why

Ephesians 1 speaks of "every spiritual blessing" as already ours in Christ.

God's Plan from Eternity

The phrase "before the foundation of the world" emphasizes God's eternal purpose. This was not a backup plan after humanity sinned; it was His plan all along to redeem a people through Christ and to display His glory through them. As Paul will later say, God's intent was "that now unto the principalities and powers in heavenly places might be known by the church the manifold wisdom of God" (Eph. 3:10, KJV).

Seen this way, predestination is about God's sovereign plan, but the plan's goal is corporate witness and mission. Just as a Greek or Roman colony was planned and populated intentionally to extend the home city's influence, God has planned and populated His Colony of Heaven to extend His kingdom's influence on earth.

Privilege vs. Purpose

Misreading predestination as privilege leads to spiritual pride or despair: pride for those who believe they're chosen elites, despair for those who fear they're left out. But reading predestination as purpose leads to mission, humility, and assurance. If you are in Christ, you are chosen for holiness and adoption — your future is secure, and your calling is clear. This view also preserves human responsibility. The call of the gospel goes out universally: "Whosoever will, let him take the water of life freely" (Rev. 22:17, KJV).

Practical Implications for the Colony of Heaven

1. Identity with Humility – We are chosen for God's glory, not our own. This should make us grateful, not arrogant.

2. Mission with Confidence – As ambassadors of heaven, we know our role is part of God's eternal plan.

3. Holiness with Purpose – Our predestination is unto holiness; therefore, our lifestyle matters.

4. Assurance with Hope – If you are in Christ, your adoption is secure. God's eternal plan cannot fail.

Answering Common Objections

• *"Doesn't this deny God's sovereignty?"*

No. God sovereignly determined that all who are in Christ would share His blessings and calling. He sovereignly set the destination for those in His Son.

• *"Doesn't this make salvation depend on me?"*

No. Salvation is by grace through faith (Eph. 2:8–9). We do not choose ourselves; we respond to God's call. But God's choice is about the goal and purpose, not arbitrary favoritism.

- *"Is this just corporate, not individual?"*

Corporate election includes individuals. Every believer personally shares the blessings of Christ because he or she belongs to the body chosen in Christ.

Living the Doctrine

Think again of your main metaphor. Roman colonists weren't sent to new territories for leisure; they were sent for a mission. They had privileges—land grants, citizenship, legal protections—but those privileges served a purpose: extending the empire's culture, law, and power. Likewise, God's predestination grants believers spiritual blessings for the purpose of extending His kingdom through their lives.

If we treat predestination as a privilege, we hoard it. If we treat it as a purpose, we live it out.

Closing Reflection

Predestination in Ephesians is not a mystery to fear or a weapon to argue over but a window into God's eternal plan to create a people who embody His holiness, enjoy His adoption, and extend His kingdom. It is both a comfort and a commissioning. As citizens of heaven's colony, we stand secure in God's eternal purpose and sent on His eternal mission.

Suggested Reflection Questions

5. How does seeing election as "in Christ" rather than "individual before Christ" change your understanding of Ephesians 1:4–5?

6. In what ways does predestination as purpose (rather than privilege) challenge your view of Christian life and mission?

7. How can you live out your "adoption" in Christ this week in your relationships, work, or ministry?

8. Does this view give you greater assurance or greater responsibility—or both? How?

Appendix B: The Renewed Mind: Sober Thinking and the Helmet of Salvation

In our journey through Ephesians, we've seen the church as a Colony of Heaven, an outpost of God's kingdom displaying His glory to earth and the heavens (Eph. 3:10, KJV). Central to this calling is the transformation of the believer, not just in actions but in the very way we think. Ephesians 4:17–32, the heart of Chapter 5, contrasts the futile, darkened mind of the Gentiles with the renewed mind of the believer, called to "put off" the old man and "be renewed in the spirit of your mind" (Eph. 4:17–18, 23, KJV). This renewal is no mere adjustment; it's a radical reorientation, a new worldview crafted by the Word and the Spirit. Paul uses the term "sober" in his writings to describe this disciplined, truth-anchored thinking, and he employs the powerful metaphor of the "helmet of salvation" to depict the mind's protection in Christ (Eph. 6:17). As citizens of heaven's colony, our renewed minds enable us to see the world through God's lens, living distinctly and displaying His truth. This appendix explores how the Word and the Spirit produce this sober, protected mind, transforming our understanding of truth and the world around us.

The Sober Mind in Paul's Writings

Paul's call to a renewed mind in Ephesians 4:23 echoes his broader teaching on how believers think. In several letters, he uses the Greek word *sōphroneō*, often translated "sober" in the KJV, to describe a mind that is sound, disciplined, and aligned with God's truth. For example, in Titus 2:2, he urges aged men to be "sober, grave, temperate" (KJV), and in Titus 2:5, women are to be "sober, chaste, keepers at home" (KJV). In Romans 12:3, he exhorts believers "not to think of himself more highly than he ought to think; but to think soberly" (KJV). The word *sōphroneō* carries the idea of sound-mindedness, a disciplined thought life that rejects the world's distorted reasoning (O'Brien, 1999). Unlike the Gentiles in Ephesians 4:17, whose "vanity of their mind" and "darkened understanding" lead to futility (KJV), the sober mind is anchored in God's reality. As I shared in my sermon, it's the opposite of "garbage in, garbage out." The unregenerate mind, clouded by a calloused heart (*pōrōsis*), cannot see truth clearly (Eph. 4:18; Hoehner, 2002). But the believer, taught by Christ (Eph. 4:20–21), receives a sound mind, able to discern God's will and live as His colony.

This sober thinking transforms our worldview. The world sees life through a lens of self-interest, chasing fleeting desires that promise life but deliver death, as we saw in Chapter 5. The sober mind, renewed by

God, sees through the deceitful lusts, recognizing that true life is found in Christ alone. It's a mind that weighs decisions against eternity, not momentary pleasure, equipping us to live as heaven's outpost in a fallen world.

The Helmet of Salvation

Paul extends this imagery in Ephesians 6:17, urging believers to "take the helmet of salvation" (KJV) as part of the armor of God. He uses a similar metaphor in 1 Thessalonians 5:8: "But let us, who are of the day, be sober, putting on the breastplate of faith and love; and for an helmet, the hope of salvation" (KJV). The helmet protects the head—the seat of thought and decision-making—shielding the mind from the enemy's lies and doubts. In the Roman world, a soldier's helmet was not just defensive but a symbol of identity, marking him as part of his legion (Bruce, 1984). For believers, the helmet of salvation is our assurance in Christ, guarding our minds against the world's futile thinking and Satan's accusations. It anchors us in the certainty of our redemption, freeing us to think clearly and live boldly as God's colony.

The helmet of salvation connects directly to sober thinking. In 1 Thessalonians 5:8, Paul links "sober" (sōphroneō) with the hope of salvation, suggesting that a sound mind rests in the confidence of God's saving work. This hope protects us from despair, fear, or the temptation to conform to the world's darkened understanding (Rom. 12:2). As citizens of heaven's colony, we wear this helmet not just to survive but to stand firm, displaying Christ's victory in our thoughts and actions.

The Word and the Spirit's Transformative Work

How does this renewed mind—sober and protected—come about? Through the Word of God and the Spirit of God working in tandem. The Word is our foundation: "Thy word is a lamp unto my feet, and a light unto my path" (Ps. 119:105, KJV). Scripture reveals God's truth, exposing the world's lies and reorienting our perspective. Romans 12:2 urges us, "Be not conformed to this world: but be ye transformed by the renewing of your mind, that ye may prove what is that good, and acceptable, and perfect, will of God" (KJV). The Word recalibrates our thinking, like a compass pointing true north, guiding us to see life as God does—eternal, purposeful, and centered on His glory.

The Holy Spirit brings this Word to life. Jesus promised, "When he, the Spirit of truth, is come, he will guide you into all truth" (John 16:13, KJV). Paul echoes this in 1 Corinthians 2:10–12: "The Spirit searcheth all things, yea, the deep things of God... that we might know the things that are freely given to us of God" (KJV). The Spirit illuminates Scripture, making its truths alive in our hearts and reshaping our worldview. Where the world sees chaos, the Spirit shows us God's sovereign plan. Where the world sees despair, the Spirit reveals hope in Christ's redemption. This transformed worldview enables us to live as heaven's colony, reflecting God's truth in a world of futility.

Think about a sailor lost at sea, navigating by a broken compass that spins wildly, leading him in circles. The world's thinking is like that compass— unreliable, driven by shifting desires. But the Word and the Spirit are a recalibrated compass, fixed on God's truth, guiding us through life's storms. Or picture a Roman soldier, his helmet gleaming in the sun, not just shielding his head but marking him as Rome's own. The helmet of salvation does the same for us, protecting our minds and declaring our identity in Christ. These images remind us: a renewed mind isn't passive; it's an active surrender to the Word and Spirit, equipping us to live soberly and shine as God's outpost.

Application: Living with a Renewed Mind

As citizens of heaven's colony, we are called to immerse ourselves in the Word and yield to the Spirit, allowing God to reshape our minds. This isn't a one-time event but a daily discipline. Are you reading Scripture, letting it expose the world's lies and renew your perspective? Are you praying for the Spirit to guide your thoughts, guarding you with the helmet of salvation? A renewed mind sees the world differently: where others see scarcity, we see God's provision; where others chase fleeting pleasures, we pursue eternal purpose. This sober thinking strengthens the body, enabling us to speak truth, forgive generously, and labor selflessly, as we saw in Chapter 5. Like Roman colonists transforming their regions with Rome's culture, our renewed minds display heaven's truth, making Christ's kingdom visible (Boardman, 1980).

Closing Challenge

Examine your mind: Is it clouded by the world's futility, or is it sober, protected by the helmet of salvation? Commit to the Word daily, letting it recalibrate your compass. Yield to the Spirit, who forms Christ's image in you. As you do, your worldview will shift, and you'll live as a citizen of heaven's colony, displaying God's truth to a watching world and heavenly beings.

Reflection Questions

1. How is the world's futile thinking influencing your mind, and what Scripture can you read daily to renew your perspective as a citizen of heaven's colony? (Eph. 4:17–18, KJV)

2. What distractions cloud your thoughts, and how can you "put on" the helmet of salvation through prayer to focus on Christ's truth? (Eph. 6:17, KJV)

3. How can you immerse yourself in God's Word and Spirit this week to transform one area of your thinking, like a compass fixed on His truth? (Ps. 119:105; John 16:13, KJV)

4. What practical step can you take to display Christ's kingdom with a renewed mind, reflecting heaven's colony to your community? (Eph. 3:10, KJV)

References

Boardman, J. (1980). *The Greeks Overseas*. Thames & Hudson.

Bruce, F. F. (1984). *The Epistles to the Colossians, to Philemon, and to the Ephesians*. Eerdmans.

Hoehner, H. W. (2002). *Ephesians: An Exegetical Commentary*. Baker Academic.

O'Brien, P. T. (1999). *The Letter to the Ephesians*. Eerdmans.

Glossary

A

Adoption — In the New Testament, God's act of bringing believers into His family with full legal rights as heirs (Eph. 1:5). In Roman culture, adoption granted the same status as natural-born children.

Aeolipile — A first-century steam device invented by Hero of Alexandria, used as an illustration of knowledge without wisdom.

Ambassador — A representative of a king or nation. Christians are called Christ's ambassadors, representing His kingdom on earth (2 Cor. 5:20).

B

Blameless — Living in such a way that does not bring reproach to Christ's name (Eph. 1:4).

C

Calling / Vocation — God's summons to believers to live as citizens of heaven's colony, embodying His kingdom here and now (Eph. 4:1).

Chosen / Election — God's decision "before the foundation of the world" that those in Christ would be holy and blameless, chosen for a purpose rather than privilege alone (Eph. 1:4).

Colony — An outpost of a greater city or kingdom. Used in the book as a metaphor for the church as heaven's outpost on earth.

Cornerstone — The first and key stone in an ancient building that set alignment and stability. Christ is the "chief cornerstone" of the church (Eph. 2:20).

D

Dispensation — A stewardship or management of God's grace; in Ephesians, Paul speaks of the "dispensation of the grace of God" given to him (Eph. 3:2 KJV).

E

Election — See "Chosen."

Earnest of Our Inheritance — The Holy Spirit given as a down payment guaranteeing believers' full future redemption (Eph. 1:14 KJV).

F

Fellowcitizens — Paul's term for Jews and Gentiles united in Christ's church (Eph. 2:19 KJV).

G

Gentiles — Non-Jewish peoples. In Ephesians, "Gentiles" refers to those formerly outside God's covenant promises but now included in Christ (Eph. 2:11–13).

H

Habitation of God — The church as God's dwelling place through the Spirit (Eph. 2:22 KJV).

Helmet of Salvation — A piece of spiritual armor symbolizing the believer's assurance and protection of the mind (Eph. 6:17).

I

Inheritance — The spiritual riches God gives to His people now and fully in the future (Eph. 1:11, 18).

J

Justification — God's legal declaration of righteousness upon the believer because of Christ's work. (Implied throughout Ephesians.)

K

Kingdom of God / Heaven's Colony — God's reign over His people, now expressed through the church and ultimately fulfilled in Christ's return.

L

Lasciviousness — KJV term for unrestrained sensuality or immorality (Eph. 4:19).

Lordship — Christ's supreme authority over the believer's life, contrasting with merely "accepting Jesus as Savior."

M

Manifold Wisdom of God — The many-faceted display of God's wisdom, shown through the unified church to heavenly beings (Eph. 3:10).

N

New Man / Old Man — Paul's image for the believer's transformation: putting off the "old man" (our sinful ways) and putting on the "new man" created in Christ (Eph. 4:22–24).

O

Outpost — Another metaphor for the church as a stationed community representing heaven on earth.

P

Predestination — God's determination beforehand that those in Christ will be adopted as His children and conformed to Christ's image (Eph. 1:5).

Principalities and Powers — Spiritual rulers or authorities, both angelic and demonic. God's wisdom is displayed to them through the church (Eph. 3:10, 6:12).

Prophets / Apostles — Foundational leaders of the early church, whose teaching (recorded in Scripture) anchors our faith (Eph. 2:20, 4:11).

R

Redemption — God's act of purchasing us out of sin's slavery through Christ's blood (Eph. 1:7).

Righteousness — Living in alignment with God's standards; a core trait of the "new man" (Eph. 4:24).

S

Saints — All believers set apart for God, not a special class of Christians (Eph. 1:1).

Sanctification — The ongoing process of being made holy in thought, word, and action (Eph. 5:26–27).

Sealed with the Spirit — The Spirit marking believers as God's own possession until the day of redemption (Eph. 1:13).

Sober Mind / Renewed Mind — Disciplined, truth-anchored thinking transformed by the Word and the Spirit (Eph. 4:23).

Spiritual Armor — The metaphor in Ephesians 6:10–18 describing believers' God-given protection for spiritual battle.

T

Temple of the Lord — The church collectively as God's dwelling, built on Christ the cornerstone (Eph. 2:21).

Trespasses and Sins — KJV language for violations of God's law and missing His standard (Eph. 2:1).

V

Vocation — Another term for calling. In Ephesians, it refers to the believer's summons to live as God's representative (Eph. 4:1).

W

Workmanship — The believer as God's "*poiēma*" or masterpiece, created in Christ Jesus for good works (Eph. 2:10).

www.ingramcontent.com/pod-product-compliance
Lightning Source LLC
Chambersburg PA
CBHW060613130626
46555CB00002B/515